ROLY'S CAFÉ & BAKERY

ROLY'S CAFÉ & BAKERY

Paul Cartwright
Paolo Tullio
Hugh Hyland
David Walsh

GILL & MACMILLAN

Gill & Macmillan Ltd
Hume Avenue, Park West, Dublin 12
with associated companies throughout the world
www.gillmacmillan.ie

© Roly's Bistro 2009
978 07171 4660 4

Index compiled by Rachel Pierce, Verba Editing House
Photographs by Neil Macdougald
Design by Orlagh Murphy
Printed by GraphyCems Ltd, Spain

This book is typeset in Schneidler 10pt.

The paper used in this book comes from the wood pulp of managed forests. For every tree felled, at least one tree is planted, thereby renewing natural resources.

A CIP catalogue record for this book is available from the British Library.

5 4 3 2

With thanks to my colleagues and fellow directors,
Hugh Hyland, John and Angela O'Sullivan.

Contents

Acknowledgment

To Neil Macdougald, photographer. Thank you for your inspiration and enthusiasm while taking the photographs in the making of this book.

Conversion Charts

Oven Temperature Conversions

Celsius	Fan oven	Fahrenheit	Gas
130°	110°	250°	½
140°	120°	275°	1
150°	130°	300°	2
160°	140°	320°	3
180°	160°	350°	4
190°	170°	375°	5
200°	180°	400°	6
220°	200°	425°	7
230°	210°	450°	8
240°	220°	475°	9

Metric–Imperial Weight Conversions

15g	½oz
25g	1oz
50g	2oz
75g	3oz
125g	4½oz
150g	5oz
175g	6oz
200g	7oz
225g	8oz
250g	9oz
275g	10oz
300g	11oz
350g	12oz
375g	13oz
400g	14oz
425g	15oz
450g	1lb
1kg	2lb 3oz
1.8kg	4lb

Metric–Imperial Liquid Conversions

25ml	1 fl oz
50ml	2 fl oz
100ml	3 fl oz
125ml	4 fl oz
150ml	5 fl oz
200ml	7 fl oz
250ml	9 fl oz
300ml	10 fl oz
325ml	11 fl oz
350ml	12 fl oz
375ml	13 fl oz
400ml	14 fl oz
450ml	15 fl oz
500ml	17 fl oz
600ml	1 pint
1 litre	1¾ pints
1.5 litres	2½ pints

Introduction   by Paolo Tullio

There are few restaurants that get past their tenth birthday –
the vast majority change their name or their owner long before
that. It's partly because restaurants are subject to trends and
some simply become unfashionable over time, but it's mainly
because few restaurants manage to keep up the enthusiasm and
drive that are needed for consistency.

Consistency is what separates the good from the bad when
it comes to restaurants. It's that relentless attention to every
small detail that's the common factor in long-lived restaurants,
and that very attention to detail is what makes for consistency.
Roly's has been going strong since 1992, which in restaurant
terms makes it some kind of Methuselah at 17. But before I get
into the history of the restaurant, let me tell you a bit about the
pre-history.

I remember well when Roly's opened in Ballsbridge in 1992.
The Celtic Tiger economy hadn't yet been thought of, much less
named, and the Ireland of those days was not a place where
disposable income was in abundance. Times were hard enough,
people were emigrating in droves and Gay Byrne used to joke
on his morning radio show, 'Would the last person leaving the
country please turn out the lights?'

That was the background against which the new Roly's opened,
a time when entrepreneurial endeavours were truly risky. Here,
partners Roly Saul, John O'Sullivan, Angela O'Sullivan, John

Mulcahy and chef Colin O'Daly had actually built themselves a restaurant from scratch – a novel idea at the time – and it was a big one at that, on two floors. It was an act of immense optimism.

Back in 1992, there were 150 restaurant seats in Ballsbridge and most of those were in Roly's. By 2006, there were over 1,300. That figure alone gives you a good idea of what the Celtic Tiger meant to the restaurant business. Looking back with 20/20 hindsight, it's obvious that having a restaurant up and running in 1992 meant you were well placed to catch the beginnings of the boom, but at the time, no one knew that boom was coming and opening a restaurant was far from a secure investment. In fact, a little like today in 2009, restaurants were closing all around the country. Mine had closed by then and so had Colin O'Daly's in Blackrock, perhaps fortuitously, because it left him free to join the Roly's team.

So much for the early years. Roly's quickly became a well-known name. The original concept, right from day one, was to have a restaurant where you could get good food at moderate prices, or in Colin O'Daly's words, 'haute cuisine at ready-to-wear prices'. It's a philosophy they've never wavered from. Even during the Wonder Years, when money seemed to be no object to anyone, Roly's kept their prices moderate. Today, their three-course lunch, properly served and eaten off a linen-clad table, is still one of the best-value meals in Dublin.

Roly's has obviously seen changes over the years. Roly Saul has gone off to open other restaurants, to the confusion of many who assume that a restaurant called 'Roly' and 'Roly's' are one and the same. Colin O'Daly no longer cooks, preferring now to follow his painting career. If he's not painting in the Aran Islands, he'll be painting in the sunnier climes of Italy.

In 1996, Paul Cartwright joined the team as head chef. He arrived with an impressive CV. Having trained in Ireland and France, he ended up in London's Savoy, cooking under their head chef, Anton Edelman, for nearly five years. That's the sort of experience that most chefs would kill for, and working in close proximity to a master means that a lot rubs off onto the younger chef. In his time there, Paul was in charge of a hundred or so chefs, so apart from cooking skills, Paul learned the organisational skills needed to run a busy restaurant. In 2000, he became the general manager of Roly's. Under his direction, the original philosophy hasn't changed and value for money is still the driving motif.

The Kitchen

A restaurant, like a game of football, is comprised of two halves, the half the public sees and interacts with – the front of house – and the part it doesn't see – the kitchen. The perfect marriage of these two halves is what makes a successful restaurant. In an ideal world, the customer need never be aware of the army of

people in the background each doing their part. All the customer needs is the seamless transition from kitchen to dining room table for a meal to be successful.

If you've never seen a restaurant kitchen in the middle of a busy service, you might be surprised at the almost military style of co-ordination. For 361 days a year, 24 chefs each do their part in producing the food for the tables, and the statistics are astounding. For example, every day, a hundredweight of potatoes is processed, while every year, over 4 tons of prawns are prepared and 26 tons of flour are used. Dealing with quantities like that needs a field marshal's ability to control logistics, as well as an accountant's awareness of detail.

The day begins early, at six in the morning, when deliveries begin to arrive and the bakery fires up the ovens. In the kitchens, the stockpots and the soups are put on the boil in huge 75-litre cauldrons. If you've ever seen a cartoon of cannibals with a missionary in the cooking pot, that's the sort of size we're looking at here. Everything you see in the kitchens dwarfs the domestic equivalent, but then, it has to – the volume of food that needs to be prepared is huge. This is a kitchen where 50 litres of stock is used daily, where pesto is made in buckets and where soups are boiled in massive cauldrons.

During the morning of frenetic activity, the supplies are coming in the back door and need to be checked against invoices and order forms. In recent years, a whole new level of bookkeeping and form-filling has come into existence, called HACCP, generally pronounced 'hassip'. It stands for Hygiene Analysis Critical Control Points, and it's a system designed to make every raw ingredient traceable back to its source. Everything is tagged, labelled by date and frequently tested by food scientists to ensure purity and quality. Again, this is a part of the catering world that the paying customer never sees, but it's there, unseen, to protect the consumer.

All of this happens daily, because everything in Roly's is bought by the day and sold by the day. That may seem like it's stating the obvious, but it's by no means the norm in the catering industry. Buying and selling food by the day means you need to have a very clear idea of your needs, or there will be mountains of waste.

Once all the supplies are in, usually by midday, the lunchtime customers begin to arrive and the culinary day begins once again. On a busy day, that means that over 350 people will be served at lunch and as many again at dinner.

The Wines

When it comes to dining, wine is integral to the meal. How restaurants choose to incorporate wine into their bills of fare varies from place to place. There's an industry standard, which is to take the cost of the bottle, multiply that by three and put that price on a wine list, though some restaurants use a multiple of four or even more. The result of that is that if you were to order a wine for €50 or more, there would be more profit for the restaurant on that bottle of wine than there would be on the whole meal.

When you compare the amount of work it takes to prepare a meal and the amount it takes to uncork a bottle, you could be forgiven for thinking that that pricing structure is not far short of insane. I remember having this conversation with John O'Sullivan many years ago, who had always been of the belief that wines ought to be fairly priced.

Roly's wine list follows its philosophy. The list contains many of the wines widely known in Ireland, so you can see at a glance that the price in Roly's is always much less than it is in other restaurants. This isn't just generosity on Roly's part; it makes good business sense. People are far more inclined to order a second bottle if they don't feel they've been ripped off on the first. The proof of the good sense of this strategy is that Roly's sells more wine than any other restaurant. In 2008, it averaged more than a 1,000 bottles a week, a truly staggering figure.

Reinvention

It's a Darwinian truth that anything that doesn't adapt to changing circumstances won't survive, and restaurants are

as subject to this truth as anything else. Changing tastes and changing habits all need to be responded to. There's no doubt that 2009 will put the ability to adapt to the test once again. The great value lunch is there as always, but for 2009 there are new initiatives. Right through the summer on Mondays and Tuesdays, a four-course dinner is on offer with wine included for €45 per person. Another initiative is the Wine Special that runs from Thursdays to Sundays, where if you buy a bottle of wine with your meal, you get a complementary one to take home with you.

The biggest change in recent years has been turning the downstairs into a café in its own right instead of keeping it as an overflow for the upstairs restaurant. It was a response to people wanting something quicker and cheaper than a full lunch, and the café supplied that need. The café has given Roly's a chance to play to their strengths. It's a place where you can drop in for a good coffee or a simple snack.

The café has made better use of the facilities that Roly's already had – a location in the heart of Dublin 4 and all the offices that are based there, and, of course, their bakery. People had always enjoyed the home-made breads that Roly's made and the breads had always been available for sale to customers at the front door, but the new café brought the bakery's range of breads and cakes to a new audience.

The Café

The café was designed to have seating at the back and a service counter and display units just inside the door. The rear part of the room was for seating, but a screen allowed it to be separated from the retail end if the space was needed at night for parties or functions when the café was closed.

Customers could now come in and buy a loaf of bread, a cake or even a ready-made meal to take away. The take-away meals were an instant hit, because what you could get was exactly the same dish that was served in the restaurant. Another innovation was that it also supplied a good breakfast, which was another new departure. Roly's is one of the few restaurants in Dublin where you can go for breakfast, lunch and dinner. Lastly, a home delivery service for the ready-made meals is now in operation, a real boon to those who now do their entertaining at home.

With up to 100 people a day served lunch in the café added to the hundreds served in the upstairs restaurant, you can see why the kitchens need to be so well managed.

The Bakery

In the early years, all the breads, cakes and desserts were made in the restaurant kitchens, but as Roly's became busier, that was no longer possible. In 1996, they made the bakery, which is at the back of the building. David Walsh is in charge – he trained

as a chef, took an advanced pastry course and then a degree in National Culinary Arts. He began his career in Roly's as chef de parti, but in 1998 took over the running of the bakery.

Up to seven bakers work here, depending on the day's workload, and just as in the kitchens, the quantities involved are large. Just to give you an idea, the bakery uses an average of 350 litres of cream a week, up to 600 litres of milk, 4,000 eggs and 70 kilos of chocolate. They use an average of half a ton of flour every week, including 11 different types of flour, ranging from gluten-free to T65, a strong flour for baguettes. All the ingredients that David uses in the bakery are organic, and no preservatives of any kind are used.

The bakery supplies both the café and restaurant as well as providing the breads and cakes for the café's off-sales. The day starts early for the bakers, before 6 a.m., when the ovens are turned on to heat up. Over the course of day, more people arrive to work as the demands on it increase, and by nine at night the ovens are still warm.

The café alone needs between 100 and 150 loaves: 20 long loaves for sandwiches, 60 brown loaves and up to 120 cakes and tarts every day of the week. The restaurant has its needs as well, requiring between six and nine varieties of bread daily, which are made into long loaves for slicing. As a customer of the restaurant, your breadbasket will normally contain four different breads. As well as the breads, the bakery makes between six and eight different desserts every day for the restaurant, and up to 120 of them.

The Recipes

The kitchens, the bakery and the front of house all combine seamlessly to bring the Roly's diner a unique experience. I hope in this introduction I've let you see why this restaurant has been a favourite of mine over the past 17 years. It's that rare combination of good food and value for money that is its essence.

Over the years, there have always been customer favourites, dishes that never fail to please. Many of these recipes are in the book *Roly's Bistro*, published in 2002. This book of recipes brings you a whole new raft of recipes, all tried and tested on the many customers Roly's has served since then. In this book, you'll find recipes that cover all ranges of skills, from the beginner to the accomplished amateur. None of them is hard to make, the recipes are easy to follow and the result will be food that's a pleasure to eat. These are recipes for everyone – they don't require special equipment or specialist skills. Think of them as a guide to more interesting food that can be made in your own kitchen.

Chapter 1

THE CAFÉ

Poached Eggs with Bacon, Tomato & Potato Cakes

Serves 4

200ml white wine vinegar

8 eggs (free range or organic)

8 slices of bacon

8 pieces of Kelly's Black Pudding (or other)

8 baby plum tomatoes

100ml olive oil

For the potato cakes:

225g potatoes, freshly boiled

1 egg yolk

35g spring onions or chives, chopped

50g flour

25g butter, melted

½ tsp salt

Note: Eggs can be poached in advance and plunged into ice water to stop them cooking, then reheated in hot water. The potato cakes should be made up to one day in advance.

1. Preheat the oven to 200°C.

2. In a large saucepan, bring about 2 litres of water to the boil, then turn down the heat. Add the vinegar and a good pinch of salt. With a spoon, mix the water in a circular motion, then break the eggs into the water, one by one. Cook for approximately 5 minutes for soft eggs.

3. To make the potato cakes, mash the freshly cooked potatoes. Add the egg yolk, spring onion or chives, flour, melted butter and salt and mix together.

4. Roll the potato mixture out into 4 circular shapes about 6mm thick, then brown on both sides on a warm greased pan for about 4 minutes on each side, until cooked.

5. Place the tomatoes on a baking try and drizzle some olive oil over them. Roast the tomatoes for 10 minutes (heating the potato cakes at the same time if you've made them in advance).

6. Meanwhile, grill the bacon and black pudding on a wire rack for approximately 3 minutes on each side.

7. Divide the poached eggs, bacon, black pudding and potato cakes between four plates and serve.

Scrambled Egg
with Smoked Salmon

Serves 4

8 slices smoked salmon

**8 eggs (free range
  or organic)**

200ml cream

50g butter

**salt & freshly ground
  black pepper**

**1 bunch chives,
  finely chopped**

**salad leaves, to garnish
  (optional)**

*Note: This dish may be served
for breakfast or as a starter for
a dinner party.*

1. Line 4 cocotte moulds or teacups with the smoked salmon. Break the eggs into a bowl, add the cream and butter and mix well to combine. Season with salt and pepper.

2. Cook the eggs on a low heat in a small, heavy-bottomed saucepan, stirring continually, until scrambled. Add the chopped chives and stir in.

3. Divide the scrambled egg between the 4 moulds and fold any remaining salmon back over. Turn onto 4 plates and garnish with mixed salad leaves.

Feta Cheese
& Spinach Omelette

Serves 1

3 eggs

salt & freshly ground
  black pepper

100ml olive oil

50g baby spinach, washed

25g feta cheese,
  cut into cubes

1. Break the eggs into a bowl, season with salt and pepper and whisk with a fork.

2. Heat the olive oil in a non-stick pan, then add the baby spinach and beaten egg. Stir vigorously on a high heat for 1 minute. Add the feta cheese and mix gently, until the egg begins to set. Fold over, turn onto a plate and serve immediately.

Carrot & Coriander Soup

1 tbsp vegetable oil

3 sticks celery, chopped

1 onion, finely diced

1 clove garlic, crushed

1 tsp ground coriander

6 large carrots,
  cut into small cubes

4 small potatoes,
  cut into small cubes

1 litre chicken stock (see p.178)

50ml cream

salt & freshly ground
  black pepper

1 bunch fresh coriander,
  chopped

1. Heat the vegetable oil in a saucepan. Add the celery, onion and garlic and cook slowly without colouring for about 10 minutes. Add the ground coriander and cook for 2 minutes. Add the carrot, potato and chicken stock, bring to the boil and simmer for 45 minutes, until all the vegetables are soft.

2. Remove from the heat and blend in a food processor. Add the cream and season with salt and pepper. Stir in the chopped coriander and serve.

French Onion Soup

Serves 4

50g butter

4 medium onions, finely sliced

25g sugar

1 litre chicken stock (see p.178)

**salt and freshly ground
    black pepper**

4 slices French bread

75g Gruyère cheese, grated

1. Melt the butter in a saucepan. Add the onions and cook slowly for about 20 minutes, until they are very soft.

2. Increase the heat and brown the onions, stirring all the time. Add the sugar and cook for 1 minute. Stir in the chicken stock, season with salt and pepper and bring to the boil. Simmer for about 30 minutes.

3. Put a slice of bread into each bowl and pour the soup over. Sprinkle with the Gruyère cheese and put under the grill or in a hot oven until the cheese is melted and bubbling, then serve.

Tomato & Basil Soup
with Goat's Cheese Croûtes

Serves 4

1 tbsp vegetable oil

2 onions, finely diced

2 cloves garlic, crushed

2 slices smoked pancetta,
  chopped into small pieces
  (optional)

900g fresh tomatoes, chopped

30g tomato purée

500ml chicken stock (see p.178)

1 bunch basil, chopped

salt and freshly ground
  black pepper

40g goat's cheese

12 slices of baguette

1. Heat the vegetable oil in a saucepan and gently cook the onions for about 10 minutes. Add the crushed garlic and cook for 5 minutes. Add the pancetta, if using, and cook for 5 minutes, then add the chopped tomatoes, tomato purée and chicken stock. Bring to the boil and simmer for about 35 minutes.

2. Remove from the heat and blend in a food processor. Pass through a sieve and add the chopped basil, seasoning to taste.

3. Spread the goat's cheese on the bread slices, then put under the grill until brown. Serve alongside the soup.

Grilled Vegetable Salad
with Roast Garlic Dressing

Serves 4

For the roast vegetables:

1 red pepper, cut into cubes

1 yellow pepper, cut into cubes

1 red onion, cut into cubes

1 clove garlic, left whole

1 sprig of thyme

1 sprig of rosemary

200ml olive oil

salt & freshly ground
  black pepper

1 medium aubergine, sliced

1 medium courgette, sliced

For the puff pastry twirls:

20g black olive purée

25g Parmesan cheese, grated

2 small garlic cloves, crushed

100g ready-to-roll puff pastry,
  rolled out to 2mm thick

For the salad:

roast garlic dressing (see p.180)

50g rocket salad

100ml balsamic vinegar

100ml olive oil

100g Parmesan cheese, flaked

1. To roast the vegetables, preheat the oven to 200°C.

2. Place the peppers, red onion, garlic, thyme and rosemary on a roasting tray. Drizzle with half the olive oil and season with salt and pepper. Cook for 15–20 minutes, until the vegetables are soft.

3. Heat the remaining olive oil in a griddle or frying pan and cook the aubergine and courgette until soft. Mix all the vegetables together, season to taste and keep warm.

4. To make the puff pastry twirls, raise the oven temperature to 220°C. Mix the black olive purée, Parmesan cheese and garlic together and spread over the puff pastry. Cut into 4 strips and twist each strip into a twirl. Place the twirls on a baking tray and cook for 10 minutes, until golden brown.

5. To serve, spoon some roast garlic dressing onto 4 plates and arrange the roasted vegetables on top. Toss the rocket salad with the balsamic vinegar and olive oil and season, then place on top of the roasted vegetables. Sprinkle with Parmesan cheese and put a puff pastry twirl on top of each plate.

Spinach & Rocket Salad with Poached Eggs,

Garlic Croutons & Bacon Dressing

Serves 4

200g baby spinach, washed

200g rocket salad, washed

60ml olive oil

2 large slices white bread, crusts removed

1 clove garlic, crushed

12 streaky bacon rashers, cut into lardons

30ml balsamic vinegar

salt & freshly ground black pepper

4 poached eggs (see p.18)

1. Put the washed baby spinach and rocket into a large salad bowl.

2. Warm half the olive oil in a frying pan. Cut the bread into 1cm cubes and add to the pan. Cook until the cubes are golden brown, then stir in the crushed garlic and cook for about 1 minute. Remove from the pan onto a warm plate.

3. Put the bacon into the pan and cook until golden brown, then remove to a warm plate.

4. Take the pan off the heat and add the balsamic vinegar and remaining olive oil. Mix well together and season to taste.

5. Toss the spinach, rocket, croutons and bacon together in the large bowl, then divide between 4 salad bowls. Top with a warm poached egg and drizzle with the oil and vinegar dressing.

Smoked Chicken Salad with Caesar Dressing

Serves 4

For the salad:

4 breasts of smoked chicken, sliced

2 heads Cos lettuce, washed & cut into 4cm pieces

½ head iceberg lettuce, washed & cut into 4cm pieces

50g Parmesan cheese, grated

For the Caesar dressing:

2 egg yolks

4 anchovies

1 clove garlic, crushed

50ml white wine vinegar

50g Parmesan cheese, grated

4 drops Worcestershire sauce

200ml sunflower oil

salt & freshly ground black pepper

1. Put the sliced smoked chicken into an ovenproof dish and warm in the oven.

2. To make the dressing, place all the ingredients except the sunflower oil into a liquidiser and blend. With the motor still running, slowly add the oil, then season with salt and pepper to taste.

3. Mix the Cos and iceberg lettuce together in a large bowl, then toss in the Caesar dressing. Divide the salad between 4 bowls and top with the smoked chicken. Sprinkle with Parmesan cheese and serve.

Goat's Cheese Tart

Serves 4

½ **pack of ready-to-roll puff pastry, cut into 4 x 13cm rounds (a saucer is a good size for this)**

400g roast vegetables (see p.29)

4 x 100g slices of chèvre (goat's cheese)

100g basil pesto (from a jar or see recipe on p.179)

100g tomato relish (see p.178)

1. Preheat the oven to 200°C.

2. Pre-cook the puff pastry bases on a baking tray for 15 minutes, until brown. When cool, place on a baking tray and place another baking tray on top to flatten to discs.

3. Lower the oven temperature to 180°C.

4. Divide the roasted veg between the 4 puff pastry bases, then place a slice of goat's cheese on each. Bake for 15 minutes, until the goat's cheese has started to melt.

5. Serve with the basil pesto and tomato relish on the side.

Crab & Ricotta Cheese Quiche

Serves 4

For the shortcrust pastry:
100g butter
200g soft flour
1 pinch of salt
2-3 tbsp water

125g ricotta cheese
200g white crab meat
2 eggs
150ml milk
150ml double cream
**salt & freshly ground
  black pepper**
25g Parmesan cheese, grated
mixed salad, to serve

1. Preheat the oven to 200°C.

2. To make the pastry, rub the butter into the flour until it resembles breadcrumbs. Add a pinch of salt. Bind with cold water.

3. Roll out the pastry and line a 20cm flan tin with it. Leave to rest in the fridge for 30 minutes. Bake blind in the oven for 10 minutes, then remove.

4. Reduce the oven temperature to 180°C.

5. Crumble the ricotta cheese into the flan case and add the crab meat. In a separate bowl, whisk together the eggs, milk and cream, season with salt and pepper and pour over the crab meat. Return to the oven and cook for about 30 minutes, until set. Halfway through cooking, sprinkle with the Parmesan cheese.

6. Serve with a salad.

Roast Beef
& Rocket Sandwich

Serves 4

For the horseradish sauce:

4 tbsp mayonnaise

**1 tbsp freshly grated
horseradish**

1 tsp chopped chives

For the sandwich:

**8 slices Roly's white yeast
bread (p.94)**

40g butter

**8 slices of roast Hereford beef,
cooked medium well**

**salt & freshly ground
black pepper**

**red onion marmalade
(see p.179)**

50g rocket salad, washed

1. To make the horseradish sauce, mix all the
ingredients together. Set aside.

2. Butter the bread and divide slices of beef between 4
slices. Season with salt and pepper and spread with the
horseradish sauce.

3. Spread 1 level tablespoon of red onion marmalade
over the sauce, then sprinkle with rocket. Cover with
the remaining slices of bread and serve.

Club Sandwich

Serves 4

**12 slices of white
   or brown bread**

15g butter

4 tbsp mayonnaise

**2 chicken breasts,
   cooked & sliced**

**2 tomatoes, sliced (plum
   are best for this)**

**½ head iceberg lettuce,
   washed & shredded**

8 rashers of bacon, grilled

2 hardboiled eggs, sliced

1. Toast the bread and butter it.

2. Set out 4 slices of the bread and spread with half the mayonnaise. Divide the chicken and the tomatoes between them, top with another slice of bread and spread the remaining mayonnaise on top.

3. Divide the lettuce and bacon between the sandwiches, top with sliced boiled egg and the last slice of bread. Cut the sandwiches into 4 triangles and serve.

Pasta with Tomatoes, Garlic, Chilli & Olive Oil

Serves 4

400ml extra virgin olive oil

2 cloves garlic, chopped

½ red chilli, chopped

20 cherry tomatoes,
  washed & dried

salt & freshly ground
  black pepper

100g rocket salad

100g basil, torn

500g cooked pasta, kept warm

100g Parmesan cheese, grated

1. Warm the olive oil in a large, heavy-bottomed pan. Add the chopped garlic and cook very slowly for about 10 minutes, then add the chopped chilli and cook for 5 minutes.

2. Add the tomatoes to the pan, season with salt and pepper and cook for a further 30 minutes, stirring occasionally, until the tomatoes are soft.

3. To serve, add the rocket, basil and warmed pasta to the pan and mix gently. Divide between 4 plates and sprinkle with grated Parmesan.

Coq au Vin
with Spring Onion Mash

Serves 4

**1 whole chicken cut for sauté
(your butcher will
do this for you)**

2 cloves garlic

1 small bunch rosemary

1 small bunch thyme

**2 carrots, peeled
& roughly chopped**

½ bottle of red wine

200ml olive oil

1 onion, finely chopped

**100g streaky rindless smoked
bacon, cut into strips**

100g button mushrooms

**salt & freshly ground
black pepper**

50g chopped parsley

For the spring onion mash:

750g potatoes, peeled

50g butter

100ml double cream

**1 bunch scallions (spring
onions), chopped**

**salt & freshly ground
black pepper**

1. Put the chicken pieces in a large bowl with the garlic, rosemary, thyme and chopped carrot. Cover with the red wine and leave in the fridge to marinate overnight.

2. Preheat the oven to 200°C.

3. Warm the olive oil in a large, heavy-bottomed, ovenproof pot. Add the onion and cook for 5–10 minutes, until soft. Add the smoked bacon and mushrooms and cook for 5–10 minutes more.

4. Remove the chicken from the marinade. Strain the wine through a fine sieve into the pot with the mushrooms and bacon.

5. Heat a separate frying pan until smoking hot. Pat the chicken dry and season with salt and pepper. Brown the chicken in the hot pan, then add to the pot with the mushrooms, bacon and wine.

6. Cover the pot and cook in the oven for approximately 1 hour, stirring occasionally.

7. Meanwhile, to make the mash, cook the potatoes in a large pot of salted water. Drain, then return to the pot and dry out on a low heat. Add the butter and cream and mash. Stir in the scallions and season with salt and pepper.

8. To serve, divide the coq au vin between 4 bowls, making sure to serve some breast and leg meat in each bowl. Spoon on the spring onion mash and sprinkle with chopped parsley.

Tomato and Basil Soup

Rolys Baked Lasagne
with mixed Leaf Salad

Thai Spiced Fishcakes
with Sweet and Sour
Chilli Dressing

Traditional Kerry Lamb
and Vegetable Pie

Chicken, Ham & Pea Lasagne

Serves 4

**4 chicken breasts,
  cooked & sliced**

200g ham, cooked & sliced

200g peas, cooked

100g Cheddar cheese, grated

12 sheets lasagne

For the tarragon velouté:

50g butter

50g plain flour

**1 litre chicken stock, hot
  (see p.178)**

200ml double cream

1 bunch tarragon, chopped

1. Preheat the oven to 200°C.

2. To make the velouté, melt the butter in a saucepan
and add the flour. Cook on a low heat without
colouring for about 5 minutes. Slowly add the
chicken stock, stirring all the time, until all stock is
incorporated. Simmer, still stirring, for 5 minutes. Add
the double cream and chopped tarragon.

3. In a large ovenproof dish about 4cm deep, spoon in a
quarter of the tarragon sauce and spread it evenly in the
bottom of the dish. Next, add a layer of lasagne sheets,
followed by a layer of chicken, ham and peas. Repeat
three times, finishing with a layer of sauce.

4. Sprinkle the top with the grated Cheddar and cook
for 30–35 minutes, until the lasagne is hot the whole
way through.

Chicken, Pepper, Tomato & Basil Casserole

Serves 4

300ml olive oil

2 large onions,
  cut into 2cm cubes

3 garlic cloves, crushed

1 red pepper, cut into 2cm cubes

1 yellow pepper,
  cut into 2cm cubes

6 carrots, peeled
  & cut into 2cm cubes

100g mushrooms, sliced
  & stalks removed

2 litres chicken stock
  (see p.178)

16 small potatoes, peeled

200g cherry tomatoes

8 chicken breasts, cut into strips

1 bunch basil, chopped

salt & freshly ground
  black pepper

1. Warm the olive oil in a large saucepan. Add the onions and garlic and cook for 10 minutes without colouring. Add the peppers, carrots and mushrooms and cook for 10 more minutes without colouring.

2. Add the chicken stock, bring to the boil and simmer for 45 minutes. Then add the potatoes and simmer for another 30 minutes. Add the cherry tomatoes and chicken strips and cook for 15 minutes more. Stir in the basil, season to taste and serve.

Roast Loin of Pork with Roasted Vegetables & Apple Sauce

Serves 4

1 kg loin of pork

300g Kelly's Black Pudding (or other)

salt & freshly ground black pepper

200ml vegetable oil

400g organic root vegetables, such as carrots, parsnips, potatoes, peeled & roughly chopped

300ml olive oil

For the apple sauce:

2 apples

100ml water

1 tsp sugar

1. Preheat the oven to 220°C.

2. With a sharp knife, open a cavity in the pork loin along its length. Stuff with the black pudding, then tie with kitchen string. Season the pork with salt and pepper and place in a roasting tray. Pour over the vegetable oil, then put into the preheated oven for 20 minutes.

3. Reduce the heat to 190°C and cook for a further 50 minutes, turning the pork over after 25 minutes.

4. Place all the vegetables in a separate roasting tray, season with salt and pepper and pour over the olive oil. Cook for 50 minutes along with the pork, turning occasionally until done.

5. Meanwhile, to make the apple sauce, peel and core the apples, then cut into small pieces. Place in a saucepan with the water and sugar and cook on a gentle heat for 15 minutes, until the apples are soft. Remove to a blender and purée until smooth.

6. Remove the pork from the oven and leave to rest for 10 minutes. Remove the string, carve and serve surrounded by the roasted vegetables and apple sauce.

Fish Pie.

¼ **litre white wine**

½ **litre water**

200ml white wine vinegar

**salt & freshly ground
  black pepper**

100g salmon, cubed

100g haddock or cod, cubed

¼ **litre milk**

**100g smoked haddock
  or smoked cod, cubed**

100g mussel meat

2 hardboiled eggs (optional)

1 litre fish cream (see p.177)

1 bunch chopped chives

**300g spring onion mash
  (see p.44)**

*Note: You may use whatever
fish you like. These are just
suggestions and what we use
in the restaurant.*

1. Preheat the oven to 200°C.

2. To cook the unsmoked salmon and haddock, bring
the white wine, water and vinegar to the boil and season
with salt and pepper. Put the salmon in the liquid and
poach for 8 minutes, until just cooked. Remove to a tray.
Repeat with the haddock and allow to cool.

3. Heat the milk in a pot and poach the smoked haddock
for 8 minutes, until cooked. Remove to a tray to cool.

4. Divide all the fish and the mussels equally between
four ovenproof bowls (or one large ovenproof dish). Put
half a boiled egg into each bowl. Ladle over the cold fish
cream, sprinkle with chopped chives and pipe on the
mashed potato. Cook for 20–25 minutes, until the pie
is heated through.

*Note: This dish may be prepared one day in advance
and kept refrigerated.*

Smoked Haddock Risotto with Parmesan

Serves 4

1 litre chicken or fish
  stock (see pp.177, 178)

100ml olive oil

1 onion, finely diced

1 clove garlic, crushed

250g arborio rice

½ glass white wine

150g cooked smoked
  haddock

30g butter

1 bunch chives,
  finely chopped

100g Parmesan

salt & freshly ground
  black pepper

1. Bring the stock to the boil in a saucepan, then set aside and keep warm.

2. Heat the olive oil in a heavy-bottomed pan. Add the onion and cook for 5 minutes, until soft, then add the garlic and cook for 2 minutes more. Add the rice and cook for about 1 minute.

3. Pour in the white wine and enough stock to cover the rice. Cook over a moderate heat, stirring frequently, adding more stock to ensure that the rice is always just covered. It will take about 15–20 minutes for the rice to be fully cooked.

4. Add the flaked smoked haddock, butter and chives and half the Parmesan. Stir and season to taste. Divide between 4 bowls or plates, sprinkle with the remaining Parmesan and serve.

Chapter 2

THE RESTAURANT

Mushroom Soup
Scented with Rosemary Truffle Cream

Serves 4

100ml vegetable oil

1 onion, finely diced

1 clove garlic, crushed

400g button mushrooms,
  washed & sliced

4 small potatoes,
  finely chopped

2 sprigs rosemary

1 litre chicken stock
  (see p.178)

salt & freshly ground
  black pepper

1 tbsp truffle oil

150ml whipped cream

1. Heat the vegetable oil in a saucepan and cook the onion gently for 10 minutes. Add the crushed garlic and cook for 5 more minutes. Add the sliced mushrooms and cook for 10 minutes, stirring occasionally.

2. Add the potato, rosemary and chicken stock and bring to the boil. Reduce the heat and simmer for approximately 35 minutes, until all the vegetables are cooked.

3. Remove from the heat and blend the soup in a food processor. Season to taste. In a separate bowl, add the truffle oil to the cream.

4. To serve, divide the soup between 4 bowls and top with the truffle cream.

Thai Spiced Fishcakes

600g floury potatoes

1 litre fish stock (see p.177)

**300g salmon fillets, skinned
& bones removed, diced**

**300g haddock fillets, skinned
& bones removed, diced**

2 tbsp vegetable oil

3 spring onions, finely chopped

**2 tbsp hot & sour tom
yum paste**

2 tbsp Thai red curry paste

2 tbsp Thai fish sauce

200ml coconut milk

1 bunch of basil, finely chopped

**1 bunch of coriander,
finely chopped**

zest & juice of 2 limes

**salt & freshly ground
black pepper**

200g flour

2 eggs, beaten

200g breadcrumbs

vegetable oil, for frying

lime wedges, to serve

1. To prepare the fishcakes, bring a large pan of salted water to the boil. Peel the potatoes and chop them into even-sized pieces. Add the potatoes to the water, bring back to boil and cook for 10 minutes. When they're done, drain the potatoes in a colander, return to the pan and let them steam dry, then mash them and leave to cool.

2. In a separate pot, bring the fish stock to the boil and gently poach the diced pieces of salmon for 4–5 minutes. Remove the salmon, then add the diced pieces of haddock to the same stock for 3–4 minutes. Remove from the stock and leave to drain and cool.

3. Meanwhile, heat the vegetable oil in a frying pan, then cook the chopped spring onions for 2 minutes. Add the tom yum paste and the red curry paste and cook for a further 2 minutes, then add the Thai fish sauce and coconut milk and leave to simmer for an additional 2 minutes.

4. When the potatoes are cool, put them into a large bowl and flake the fish into it. Add the coconut milk mixture, the finely chopped basil and coriander, lime juice and zest and a good pinch of salt and pepper. Mix everything together, remembering not to overwork the mix.

5. Dust your work surface with flour. Divide the fishcake mixture into 8 cakes about 2 cm thick, dusting them with flour as you go. Dip the fishcakes into the beaten egg and then into the breadcrumbs to coat. Place on a tray to cool for 40 minutes.

6. To cook the fishcakes, heat a thin film of vegetable oil in a hot frying pan, add the fishcakes and fry for 2–3 minutes on each side, until golden brown. Drain on kitchen paper and serve with a wedge of lime.

Mussels with White Wine,
Saffron, Cream, Garlic & Coriander

Serves 1

500ml white wine
1 onion, finely chopped
1 clove garlic, finely chopped
pinch of saffron
2kg mussels, cleaned
600ml cream
1 bunch of coriander, chopped

1. In a large saucepan, heat the white wine, onion, garlic and saffron. Add the mussels and cover with a lid. Cook the mussels on a high heat for 5–10 minutes, until they are all open; you will need to stir them 2–3 times. Any mussels that do not open should be discarded.

2. Remove the mussels from the pot and set aside. Strain the cooking liquor into a clean pot and add the cream. Bring to the boil and simmer for 3–4 minutes, then return the mussels, add the chopped coriander and serve.

Smoked Salmon
& Asparagus Salad with
Orange, Lemon & Saffron Dressing

Serves 4

12 asparagus spears

2 blood oranges

1 lemon

pinch of saffron

100ml olive oil

50ml white wine vinegar

salt & freshly ground
  black pepper

200g mixed salad, washed

8 slices of good-quality
  smoked salmon

1. Cook the asparagus in a large saucepan of boiling, salted water for approximately 4 minutes, until just cooked – there should be a little bit of a bite in the asparagus. Set aside.

2. Segment one of the blood oranges and the lemon. Squeeze the juice from the second orange and add the saffron to it. In a separate bowl, mix the olive oil and vinegar together and season with salt and pepper.

3. Dress the salad with half the oil and vinegar dressing and divide between 4 plates. Top with the smoked salmon and asparagus.

4. Mix the remaining dressing with the orange and saffron juice. Add the orange and lemon segments directly to the dressing and spoon around the salad. Serve.

Roast Fillet of Brill with Asparagus & Sauce Vierge

Serves 4

12 asparagus spears

100ml olive oil

4 x 150g brill fillets
(or fish of choice)

salt & freshly ground
black pepper

25g butter

juice of ½ lemon

For the sauce vierge:

400ml extra virgin olive oil

100ml balsamic vinegar

100g black olives, cut in half

100g green olives, cut in half

2 shallots, finely diced

1 clove garlic

10 cherry tomatoes, cut in half

salt & freshly ground
black pepper

1 bunch of chives, chopped

1. To make the sauce vierge, whisk the olive oil and vinegar together, then add the remaining ingredients except the chives, mixing well. Season with salt and pepper to taste. Warm in a pot and add the chopped chives.

2. Cook the asparagus in a large saucepan of boiling salted water for approximately 4 minutes, until just cooked – there should be a little bit of a bite in the asparagus.

3. Heat the olive oil in a frying pan until smoking hot. Season the fish with salt and pepper and place into the pan. Reduce the heat to low and cook the fish for 2 minutes. Add the butter to the pan and turn the fish over. Cook for a further 2 minutes, spooning butter over the fish occasionally. Add the lemon juice.

4. To serve, divide the asparagus between 4 plates, place the fish on top and spoon the warm sauce vierge around.

Note: Sauce vierge goes well with fish and poultry.

Roast Fillet of Hake with Minted Peas à la Françoise

Serves 4

50g butter

1 onion, finely diced

200ml white wine

½ litre chicken stock
  (see p.178)

¼ head of iceberg lettuce,
  shredded

150g cooked peas

½ bunch of mint,
  torn into pieces

100ml olive oil, for frying

4 x 180g hake fillets
  (nearly all types of fish
  work with this dish)

salt & freshly ground
  black pepper

1. Melt the butter in a saucepan, then sweat the onion in the butter until soft, without colouring. Add the white wine and reduce by half, then add the chicken stock and reduce by one-third. Add the lettuce, peas and mint and keep warm.

2. Heat the olive oil in a non-stick pan. Season the fish and put it in the pan, skin side down. Cook for about 4 minutes on each side.

3. To serve, divide the minted peas between 4 plates and put the fish on top.

Tian of Crab with Apple

200g white Castletownbere crabmeat

50g mayonnaise

50g chives, chopped

100g apple, diced

salt & freshly ground black pepper

200ml olive oil

100 ml cider vinegar

4 tomatoes, skinned, deseeded & quartered (see note)

mixed salad or rocket, to serve

Note: To skin tomatoes, first remove the stalk from the tomatoes. Put the tomatoes into a pot of boiling water for 8 seconds, then transfer into a bowl of ice water to cool, then slip off the skins. Cut into 4 segments and remove the seeds.

1. Mix the crabmeat, mayonnaise, chopped chives and half the diced apple together. Season to taste with salt and pepper.

2. Mix the olive oil and cider vinegar together, then add in the remaining apple.

3. Place 4 x 5cm pastry cutters on a tray if you are preparing these in advance, or else directly onto the plate if you will be serving this straight away. Place some of the skinned and deseeded tomato in the base of each. Top with the crab mixture and press down. Carefully remove the pastry cutters, spoon around the dressing and serve straight away.

Scallops with Roast Vegetables, Basil & Lime Dressing

Serves 4

100ml olive oil

12 large scallops

salt & freshly ground
  black pepper

25g butter

½ lemon

4 portions roast vegetables
  (see p.29), kept warm

For the basil and lime dressing:

2 egg yolks

1 tsp Dijon mustard

1 tsp honey

400ml olive oil

zest & juice of 1 lime

2 tsp basil pesto (see p.179)

1. To make the dressing, whisk the egg yolks and mustard in a bowl. Add the honey and slowly whisk in the olive oil. When all the olive oil has been incorporated, add the lime zest and juice and the pesto. Set aside.

2. Heat the olive oil in a frying pan until smoking hot. Season the scallops with salt and pepper and place into the pan one by one. Cook them for approximately 1 minute on a very high heat, then turn them over and cook for 1 more minute.

3. Turn down the heat and add the butter. When the butter has melted, add the lemon juice and spoon it over the scallops.

4. To serve, divide the roast vegetables and scallops between 4 plates. Divide the dressing between 4 shot glasses or serve in a sauceboat.

Grilled Fillet of Beef with a Ratatouille Pesto,
Parmesan Cheese Crust & Red Wine Jus

Serves 4

For the ratatouille:

100ml olive oil

1 onion, finely diced

1 clove garlic, crushed

1 red pepper, finely diced

1 yellow pepper, finely diced

½ aubergine, finely diced

1 tomato, finely chopped

1 tsp tomato purée

salt & freshly ground
  black pepper

For the red wine jus:

100ml vegetable oil

2 shallots, finely chopped

1 clove garlic, chopped

1 carrot, finely chopped

1 stick celery, finely chopped

1 glass of red wine

1 litre beef stock (see p.176)

For the beef:

4 x 6oz fillets of beef

salt & freshly ground
  black pepper

4 tsp basil pesto (see p.179)

50g Parmesan cheese, grated

Note: The ratatouille and pesto can be made up to 2 days in advance, while the red wine jus can be made and frozen in advance.

1. To make the ratatouille, warm the olive oil in a saucepan, then add the onion and garlic and cook slowly for 5 minutes. Add the diced peppers and cook for a further 5 minutes. Add the aubergine and cook for 5 more minutes, then add the tomato and tomato purée and cook for about 10 more minutes, until all the vegetables are soft. Season with salt and pepper and keep warm.

2. Meanwhile, to make the red wine jus, heat the oil in a saucepan, add the vegetables and cook for about 5 minutes, until brown, stirring occasionally. Add the wine and simmer until reduced by two-thirds. Add the beef stock and continue simmering until it has reduced by half and coats the back of a spoon. Strain through a fine sieve and keep warm.

3. Heat a griddle or frying pan until very hot. Season the beef fillets with salt and pepper. Place into the pan and sear on each side for about 2 minutes, until nice and pink.

4. To serve, put a spoonful of warm ratatouille on top of each fillet. Drizzle with the pesto and sprinkle on some of the grated Parmesan cheese. Glaze under a hot grill for about 2 minutes, until the cheese begins to bubble and turn golden brown. Serve with a little of the red wine jus poured around.

Roast Rack of Lamb with a Herb Crust,
Green Beans & Roasted Garlic

Serves 4

**4 racks of lamb,
  French trimmed**

**salt & freshly ground
  black pepper**

2 bulbs of garlic

200g green beans

25g chopped parsley

25g chopped chives

25g chopped thyme

100g breadcrumbs

2 tsp Dijon mustard

**roast vegetables, to serve
  (see p.29)**

1. Preheat the oven to 200°C.

2. Season the lamb with salt and pepper and seal in a hot pan until golden brown. Transfer to a roasting tray. Cut the bulbs of garlic in half and place in the roasting tray along with the lamb. Cook the lamb and garlic in the oven for approximately 35 minutes for medium lamb.

3. Meanwhile, cook the green beans in boiling water for 4–5 minutes, then transfer them into a bowl of ice water to stop them cooking. Drain and set aside.

4. To make the herb crust, mix all the herbs and breadcrumbs together and season with salt and pepper.

5. Remove the lamb from oven after 35 minutes and leave on a warm plate to rest for 10 minutes. Keep the garlic warm in the oven. Brush the fat side of the lamb with the Dijon mustard and cover with the breadcrumb mix, making sure to press the crumbs on firmly.

6. Put the lamb under the grill, until the breadcrumbs are golden brown.

7. To serve, heat the green beans and divide between 4 warm plates. Put half a bulb of roast garlic on each plate. Carve the lamb into 4 cutlets and place on the plates. Serve with roast vegetables.

Roast Breast of Duck with Stir-fried Noodles, Soy & Sesame Dressing

Serves 4

4 x 8oz duck breasts

**salt & freshly ground
  black pepper**

vegetable oil, for frying

For the stir-fried noodles:

200ml groundnut oil

1 onion, finely sliced

1 clove garlic, crushed

30g grated fresh ginger

1 red pepper, finely sliced

1 yellow pepper, finely sliced

½ red chilli

**2 pak choi heads, cut into
  about 6 pieces each**

50g bean sprouts

200g cooked egg noodles

**salt & freshly ground
  black pepper**

For the soy and sesame dressing:

1 tsp honey

**200ml soy sauce
  (Kikkoman's is best)**

400ml sesame seed oil

25g toasted sesame seeds

1. Preheat the oven to 200°C.

2. Score the skin of the duck breast with a sharp knife (this helps the skin go crispy during cooking) and season the breasts with salt and pepper.

3. Add a little vegetable oil to a frying pan and heat until it's smoking hot. Put the duck breasts into the pan, meat side down, and cook for 2 minutes, until sealed and brown. Turn the breasts onto the skin side, reduce the heat to medium and cook for about 5 minutes, until the skin goes crispy. Transfer to a baking tray and cook in the oven for 7 minutes. Remove from the oven and rest for 5 minutes.

4. In a wok or a large frying pan, heat the oil until smoking hot. In quick succession, add the onion, garlic, ginger, peppers, chilli, pak choi and bean sprouts, stirring all the time. After cooking on a high heat for about 2–3 minutes, stirring continuously, add the cooked egg noodles and warm through. Season with salt and pepper.

5. To make the dressing, whisk the honey and soy sauce together. Whisk in the sesame seed oil and add the sesame seeds.

6. To serve, divide the stir-fried noodles between 4 plates. Slice the duck breasts lengthways and arrange on top of the noodles, then drizzle with the sesame dressing.

Roast Loin of Venison
with Creamed Cabbage
& Juniper Berry Jus

Serves 4

4 x 150g pieces loin of venison

300ml red wine

6 juniper berries

1 sprig rosemary

1 sprig thyme

2 bay leaves

60g butter

4 portions creamed cabbage
  (see p.84)

1. Marinate the venison in the red wine, juniper berries, rosemary, thyme and bay leaves for 12–24 hours.

2. Preheat the oven to 200°C.

3. Remove the venison from the marinade and pat dry on kitchen paper. Keep the marinade to one side.

4. In a hot pan, seal the venison on all sides until brown. Cook in the oven, 20 minutes for medium rare, 35 minutes for well done.

5. Remove the venison from the oven and set aside on a warm plate. Drain the cooking pan of all grease and add the marinade. Reduce by two-thirds and strain through a fine sieve. Whisk in the butter.

6. To serve, divide the creamed cabbage between 4 plates. Slice the venison and arrange on top of the cabbage, then spoon over the sauce.

Creamed Cabbage

1 head Savoy cabbage, shredded

1 onion, finely sliced

1 carrot, finely diced

½ celeriac, finely diced

200ml cream

30g butter

**salt & freshly ground
    black pepper**

1. In a small saucepan, melt the butter, add the onions and cook until soft without allowing them to colour.

2. Add the carrot and cook for 5 minutes, then add the celeriac and cook for 10 minutes until the celeriac is soft. Add the cream and reduce by half.

3. In a separate saucepan, cook the cabbage in boiling salted water for about 5 minutes. Drain cabbage and refresh in cold water. Then squeeze the cabbage in a cloth to remove as much liquid as possible, add to the cream mixture and season to taste.

Chapter 3

The Bakery

Yeast Dough

Before dealing with or thinking about using yeast, there are a few important points to follow and understand.

The process of yeast fermentation is complicated and there are many factors that can affect the outcome of your product, but for a simple crash course, follow these rules and you'll be fine.

You have to first understand and respect that yeast is a living micro-organism. When treated correctly, it will multiply and flourish, but when treated incorrectly, it will die. Just remember – it's alive!

Yeast requires four main ingredients to survive and flourish: food, warmth, moisture and time.

1. Food
Yeast requires some sugar (glucose) before it can ferment. Wheat flour naturally contains some sugars, but to speed up and help the process along, we add more.

2. Warmth
The optimum temperature for yeast to activate and multiply, creating carbon dioxide for your bread to become aerated, is 21°–29°C (or 70°–85°F). This is crucial to achieve the best results – don't be tempted to increase temperatures, or you'll kill the yeast.

3. Moisture

Because yeast can come in block or dried form, it has to be given moisture or water to reconstitute itself, and because we use water in bread making, we can incorporate it this way. We can also control temperature in the process.

4. Time

A perfect dough is one in which the yeast has been allowed to achieve its optimum bulk and flavour – characteristics that make great bread when all these processes come into play correctly.

A complicated enzyme change occurs as the dough rises, creating carbon dioxide, fermentation, elasticity and plasticity, meaning the dough can be pulled, kneaded and shaped.

So make a cup of coffee, read the paper and relax, and give your bread the time it deserves.

Makes 2 loaves

White Soda Bread

900g cream flour
2 tsp salt
2½ tsp bread soda
750ml buttermilk,
  at room temperature

Note: To make a fruit and cherry soda bread, add 50g sugar, 100g sultanas and 100g chopped cherries, adding extra buttermilk if needed to bind the mixture. Also, for light brown soda bread, reduce the flour by 100g and add an equivalent amount of bran to the mix instead.

A very popular bread on these shores, soda bread has been found in different variations throughout Ireland, mainly from recipes handed down from generation to generation. The name is taken from the raising agent used to make this simple bread, bicarbonate of soda or bread soda.

1. Preheat the oven to 200°C.

2. In a large bowl, sieve the flour, salt and bread soda together. Repeat this step once more.

3. Make a well in the centre of the bowl and, using your hand like a paddle, start to mix the flour with the buttermilk. Mix confidently, but don't overmix.

4. When all the buttermilk has been added and you have a well-mixed dough, turn it out onto a floured surface. Next, flour your clean hands and cut the dough into 2 equal pieces.

5. Roll each piece into a separate ball and push down so they aren't too high. Place each ball on a lightly greased baking tray, then mark a cross on top of each using a sharp knife.

6. Place in the oven for 35–45 minutes, until fully baked. Remove from the oven and place on a wire cooling rack.

Roly's Brown Bread with Sunflower & Pumpkin Seeds

Makes 2 loaves

30g bread soda, sieved

375g strong white flour

**250g extra coarse
   wholemeal flour**

80g pinhead oats

80g oat flakes

80g wheat germ

20g brown sugar

1 tsp salt

1 egg, beaten

50g sunflower seeds

50g pumpkin seeds

**850ml buttermilk,
   at room temperature**

1. Preheat the oven to 200°C.

2. Using a deep bowl, sieve the bread soda and white flour together, then mix in the wholemeal flour, pinhead oats, oat flakes, wheat germ, sugar, salt, egg and seeds, making sure all the ingredients are dispersed evenly.

3. Add the buttermilk and mix well, until everything is bound together.

4. Divide the dough into 2 well-greased loaf tins and bake for 75–90 minutes, until the bread has risen and is fully baked. Turn out and pat the bottom of each loaf – if it has a hollow sound, it's fully baked. Allow the bread to cool before cutting it – if you can!

Simple White Pan

Makes 2 loaves

**750g strong white flour,
  plus extra for dusting**

1 tsp salt

2 tsp sugar

**30g fresh yeast
  (or 10g dried yeast; see note
  if using dried yeast**

**430ml tepid water
  (not above 29°C)**

20ml milk

1 egg yolk, beaten

25g unsalted butter

**poppy and/or sesame seeds
  (optional)**

*Note: Dried yeast does not
require the first proving.
If using dried yeast all the
ingredients are added in the
first mixing. When the mixing
is finished, shape into 2 loaves
straight away and leave to
prove until the dough has
doubled in size.*

1. Using a mixer with a dough hook, sieve the flour, salt and sugar together in a mixing bowl.

2. In a separate bowl, mix the yeast with the water, milk and egg yolk, making sure the yeast is fully broken down. The liquid should turn a pale grey.

3. Gradually add the liquid and butter into the flour, increasing the speed of the mixer until it forms a dough. This should take about 7–10 minutes (double the time if mixing by hand). Turn off the mixer, cover the bowl with a damp cloth and leave to prove for 40 minutes to 1 hour in a warm, draught-free place until it doubles in size.

4. Preheat the oven to 210°C.

5. Remove the cloth and mix the dough again until all the air is knocked out. Remove the dough from the bowl and divide it in half. Shape into 2 round loaves or place into 2 lightly greased baking tins. Dust the top of each with flour and poppy and/or sesame seeds, if using.

6. Allow to prove in a warm place, covered with a cloth, for about 30 minutes, until the dough has nearly reached the top of the baking tins.

7. Cook for 30–40 minutes, until the loaves are fully baked and sound hollow when tapped on the bottom.

Makes 2 loaves

Curry & Coconut Bread

750g strong white flour

25g unsalted butter

2 tsp sugar

1 tsp salt

**30g fresh yeast
(or 10g dried; see note if
using dried yeast)**

430ml tepid water

4 tsp milk

1 egg yolk

**1 tbsp cumin seeds,
plus extra for garnish**

1 tsp coriander seeds

2 tsp turmeric

2 tbsp curry paste

75g flaked coconut

**1 egg + 4 tbsp milk,
for the egg wash**

*Note: Dried yeast does not
require the first proving. If using
dried yeast, all the ingredients
are added in the first mixing,
including the seeds, turmeric,
curry paste and coconut. When
the mixing is finished, shape
into 2 loaves straight away and
leave to prove until the dough
has doubled in size.*

1. Using a mixer with a dough hook, sieve the flour into the bowl on the lowest speed, adding the butter, sugar and salt.

2. In another bowl, mix the yeast with the water, milk and egg yolk, making sure the yeast is fully broken down. The liquid should turn a pale grey.

3. Gradually add the liquid into the flour, increasing the speed of the mixer until it forms a dough. This should take about 7–10 minutes (double the time if mixing by hand). Turn off the mixer. If you're using fresh yeast, cover the bowl with a clean, damp cloth and leave to prove in a warm, draught-free place for 40 minutes to 1 hour. If you're using dried yeast, see the note below.

4. Preheat the oven to 220°C.

5. Remove the cloth and mix the dough again until all the air is knocked out. Mix in the seeds, turmeric, curry paste and coconut until a ball of dough is formed again.

6. Remove the dough from the bowl and divide it in half. Shape into 2 round loaves or put into 2 lightly oiled tins and place on baking trays. Brush with egg wash and sprinkle with cumin seeds. Cut straight across the tops of the loaves at an angle using a sharp knife and leave in a warm place, covered with a tea towel, for about 20–30 minutes, until doubled in size.

7. Place in the oven and bake for 30 minutes, putting a bowl of water in the bottom of the oven to prevent a skin forming on the bread.

Makes 2 loaves

Bacon & Onion Thyme Bread

750g strong white flour

25g unsalted butter

25g sugar

1 tsp salt

30g fresh yeast
  (or 10g dried; see note if
  using dried yeast)

430ml tepid water

4 tbsp milk

1 egg yolk

200g bacon,
  cooked & chopped

150g onion, finely diced
  & sautéed

2 tsp chopped
  fresh thyme

pinch of sea salt,
  to garnish

1 egg + 4 tbsp milk,
  for the egg wash

*Note: Dried yeast does not
require the first proving. If using
dried yeast, all the ingredients
are added in the first mixing,
including the bacon and onion.
When the mixing is finished,
shape into 2 loaves straight
away and leave to prove until
the dough has doubled in size.*

1. Using a mixer with a dough hook, sieve the flour into the bowl on the lowest speed, adding the butter, sugar and salt.

2. In another bowl, mix the yeast with the water, milk and egg yolk, making sure the yeast is fully broken down. The liquid should turn a pale grey.

3. Gradually add the liquid into the flour, increasing the speed of the mixer until it forms a dough. This should take about 7–10 minutes (double the time if mixing by hand). Turn off the mixer. If you're using fresh yeast, cover the bowl with a clean, damp cloth and leave to prove for about 40 minutes to 1 hour. If using dried yeast, see the note below.

4. Preheat the oven to 220°C.

5. Remove the cloth and mix the dough again until all the air is knocked out. Mix in the bacon and onion until a ball of dough is formed again.

6. Remove the dough from the bowl and divide it in half. Shape into 2 round loaves or put into 2 lightly oiled tins and place on baking trays. Brush with the egg wash and sprinkle with sea salt. Cut straight across the tops of the loaves at an angle using a sharp knife and leave in a warm place, covered with a tea towel, for about 20–30 minutes, until doubled in size. Sprinkle the chopped thyme over.

7. Place in the oven and bake for 30 minutes, putting a bowl of water in the bottom of the oven to prevent a skin forming on the bread.

Cream Buns (Devon Splits)

37g yeast

300ml tepid water

600g strong white flour

70g unsalted butter

2 tbsp milk powder

75g sugar

75g salt

1 small egg

1 egg + 2 tbsp milk,
  for the egg wash

50g raspberry jam

100ml whipped cream

icing sugar, for dusting

*Note: To make iced buns (Swiss buns), use the ingredients and method up to * above. Mould the dough pieces into finger shapes instead and allow to prove as in step 5. Cook as in the recipe. When completely cool, dip the tops of buns into fondant or water icing (see p.160), flavoured as desired, such as strawberry fondant, or chocolate ganache (see p.169).*

1. Dissolve the yeast in the water.

2. Using a mixer with a dough hook, mix the flour, butter, milk powder, sugar and salt together on a low speed. Gradually add the water and yeast mix until a dough is formed. It should leave the sides of the bowl clean and should be smooth, elastic and shiny in appearance, with no lumps. Allow the dough to rest under a damp cloth for 1 hour in a warm, draught-free place.

3. Preheat the oven to 230°C.

4. Divide the dough into 16 portions (approximately 60g each). Mould into round shapes by placing the dough into the palm of your hand and rotating it on a lightly floured surface, which should make a round bun shape.*

5. Place the buns on a greased baking tray. Brush the buns with the egg wash, cover with a damp cloth to prevent a skin forming and allow to rise until they've nearly doubled in size.

6. Place in the oven and bake for 12–15 minutes, then move to a wire tray to cool.

7. When the buns are completely cool, cut a 2cm hole through the top of each bun. Using a teaspoon, put a dollop of raspberry jam into the hole, then pipe in some freshly whipped cream. Dust liberally with icing sugar and serve.

Brioche

60g milk

60g fresh yeast
  (or 10g dried yeast)

540g strong white flour

2 tsp salt

60g sugar

4 large eggs

150g unsalted butter

1 egg + 4 tbsp milk,
  for the egg wash

*Note: To make a sugar glaze
for the brioche buns, place 100g
caster sugar, 50ml water and
a squeeze of lemon juice into a
saucepan and bring to the boil.
A clear syrup should form. If the
syrup is too thick, thin out with
extra water.*

This is a rich yeast dough with a buttery flavour, soft in
texture and golden in colour, which should leave no
trace of butter on your fingers. We use this enriched
dough in the restaurant throughout the year for
puddings and pâtés, or simply just to sell in our café
bakery. Sometimes we add chocolate chips and orange
to heighten the flavour.

1. Warm the milk to 27°C. Place the yeast and warm milk
together in a bowl and mix lightly with a wire whisk.

2. In a mixer fitted with a dough hook, mix together
the flour, salt, sugar and eggs, then add in the yeast and
milk and mix into a well-beaten dough. Add the butter
and beat to form a silky-smooth, toughened dough.
Allow to rest under a damp cloth for 1 hour in a warm,
draught-free place.

3. Preheat the oven to 210°C.

4. Lightly grease 24 small or 3 large fluted brioche pans.
Divide the dough into pieces weighing approximately
30g each and mould into round bun shapes, then place
in the pans. Brush with the egg wash and cover with
a clean towel. Allow to prove in a warm place until
doubled in size.

5. Bake in the oven for 10 minutes, then remove from
the pans and place on a wire rack to cool. When fully
cooled, buns can be filled with cream, coated with sugar
glaze (see note) or served as a pudding.

Éclairs

For the choux pastry:

150ml water

20g sugar

60g unsalted butter

120g strong white flour

4 large free-range eggs, beaten

For the éclairs:

200ml freshly whipped double cream

200ml chocolate glaze or chocolate ganache (see p.169)

1. To make the choux pastry, bring the water, sugar and butter to the boil in a saucepan, then remove from the heat.

2. Sieve the flour onto a sheet of paper. Lift the paper with the flour on it and pour the flour into the saucepan, then mix vigorously with a wooden spoon. Return the pan to a moderate heat, stirring continuously until the mixture leaves the sides of the saucepan. Remove the mixture from the heat and allow to cool slightly.

3. Gradually add the beaten eggs, one at a time, to make a paste. The paste should be soft and retain its shape when piped.

4. Preheat the oven to 215°C.

5. Using a 1 ¼cm plain piping nozzle, pipe 10cm-long finger shapes onto a greased baking sheet. Bake for 15 minutes, until a crisp shell is formed. Leave to cool on a wire rack.

6. Split the éclairs open with a knife and fill with freshly whipped double cream. Dip the tops in chocolate glaze or chocolate ganache.

Scones

400g self-raising flour

1 tsp baking powder

pinch of salt

100g unsalted butter

100g caster sugar

180ml fridge-cold milk

**1 egg + 4 tbsp milk,
  for the egg wash**

*Note: To make fruit scones, add
120g sultanas, 30g glacé cherries
and a pinch of mixed spice.*

1. Preheat the oven to 220°C.

2. Sieve the flour, baking powder and salt together in
a mixing bowl. Rub the butter into the flour mix until
it resembles breadcrumbs. Make a well in the centre of
the flour mixture, add in the sugar and the milk and
lightly mix into the flour.

3. When a smooth dough is formed, turn the mixture
out onto a floured surface. Knead very lightly to
remove any cracks in the mixture. Roll out the dough
until it's 2cm thick, then cut out 16 rounds using a
scone cutter dipped in flour.

4. Place onto a greased baking tray, brush with egg
wash or milk and bake for 8–10 minutes, until well
risen and light golden. Remove to a wire rack to cool.

Orange Puffs with Kumquat & Mandarin Salad

Serves 6

1 x 400g sheet puff pastry

whipped cream, to serve
  (optional)

For the orange curd:
zest & juice of 2 large oranges
juice of ½ lemon
225g caster sugar
100g butter
3 egg yolks, beaten

For the meringue topping:
3 large egg whites
300g caster sugar

For the kumquat & mandarin salad:
20 kumquats, sliced
10 mandarin oranges,
  segmented

1. To make the orange curd, place all the ingredients into the top of a double boiler, or in a bowl standing over a saucepan of simmering water. Stir until the sugar has dissolved and continue heating gently for about 20 minutes, until the curd thickens. Do not boil, or the mixture will curdle. Strain through a sieve into a bowl and allow to go cold. Store in clean, airtight jars.

2. To make the meringue topping, scald all utensils with boiling water to eliminate any grease. Whisk the egg whites until stiff peaks form. Continue whisking and add two-thirds of the sugar until the meringue is very stiff and shiny. This should take about 1 minute. Stir in the remaining sugar with a spatula.

3. Preheat the oven to 220°C.

4. Roll out the puff pastry until it's 3mm thick. Cut out as many discs as possible using a round 10cm cutter. Then take another cutter, about 7 ½ cm in diameter, and cut inside the 10cm discs, creating a smaller disc inside the larger one. Use the leftover ring of pastry from the larger disc to create a lip around the edge of the 7½cm disc. When the pastry rises this will create a pocket in the middle for the curd filling.

5. Place the discs on a greased baking sheet and bake in the oven for about 15 minutes, until fully risen and

golden brown. You should be left with a case that will hold the curd inside.

6. Reduce the oven temperature to 110°C.

7. Place 1 tablespoon of curd in the middle of each case. Pipe on the meringue topping until it's level with the top of the pastry and return the baking tray to the oven for 50 minutes, until the meringue is fully cooked. Serve immediately with the mandarin salad and whipped cream (optional).

8. Any leftover meringue topping can be used to make shells or other meringue products. Store any leftover orange curd in an airtight container in the fridge.

Strawberry or Mixed Fruit Tartlet

Serves 4

For the sweet pastry:

200g soft flour

pinch of salt

100g fine caster sugar

100g unsalted butter, softened

4 large egg yolks

1 tsp vanilla essence

For the vanilla pastry cream:

4 eggs

200g caster sugar

75g white flour

10g cornflour

1 litre milk

1 vanilla pod,
  split & seeds scraped out

2 punnets of fresh strawberries
  or other mixed fruit,
  hulled & quartered

200ml apricot glaze (see p.159)

You will also need 4 individual
  flan cases for this recipe.

Note: Pastry cream can also be flavoured with alcohol, such as whiskey, rum or brandy, or with orange, praline, almond, coffee or chocolate.

Sweet pastry (or pâté sucrée) is a simple but effective pastry that is crisp, yet melting in texture, and it keeps its shape well.

1. Preheat the oven to 190°C.

2. To make the pastry, sift the flour and salt together onto a marble or cold surface. Make a well in the centre, then add the sugar, butter and egg yolks. Using your fingertips, pinch and work the mixture until well blended – this takes time, but it's well worth it. Knead the dough gently until smooth, then allow the pastry to rest in the fridge for 1 hour.

3. Roll out the pastry until it's about 2½ mm thick. Cut out discs 1¼ cm larger than your individual flan cases.

4. Grease the flan cases and line each of them with a pastry disc, then place on a baking tray. Bake blind using greaseproof paper and rice for a weight. Cook in the oven until browned. Remove the rice and paper and fully bake the tartlet shell for a further 8 minutes. Remove the cases from the baking tray and allow to cool on a wire rack.

5. To make the pastry cream, whisk the eggs and sugar together in a bowl until almost white. Mix in the flour and cornflour.

6. Boil the milk with the vanilla pod and seeds, then whisk the boiled milk into the egg mixture. Strain this mixture into a clean, heavy-based saucepan and bring to the boil, stirring constantly. Do not leave the mix unattended, as it will burn easily.

7. Cook the mixture for 2 minutes, stirring continuously, then pour into a clean bowl to cool. Sprinkle on some caster sugar to prevent a skin forming.

8. When cold, pipe into the pastry cases and garnish with strawberries or fresh fruit. Brush the apricot glaze over.

Raspberry & White Chocolate Muffins

Makes 15 x 115g muffins

200g light brown sugar

200g soft unsalted butter

85g treacle

110ml honey

3 eggs

1 tsp vanilla essence

230g soft flour

200g strong white flour

pinch of salt

1 tsp baking powder

1 tsp bread soda

120ml buttermilk

340g fresh or frozen
  raspberries

120g white chocolate,
  roughly chopped

*Note: If you like, you can
replace the raspberries with
blueberries, blackberries,
loganberries or cranberries.*

A real breakfast treat, muffins are becoming very popular and can be bought anywhere now. The word 'muffin' is derived from the German word *'Muffe'*, which is the name of a type of cake.

Muffins are baked in special tins, usually comprising 12 individual shapes. The characteristic of a good muffin is a mushroom shape and it should be very moist. The secret to success is how you add and trap the moisture. Lining the muffin tins with paper helps to keep them from drying out.

1. Preheat the oven to 140°C.

2. Line the muffin baking tin with paper cases, skipping every other space to allow the muffins enough room to mushroom on top as they bake. Grease the top of the pan so they don't stick.

3. Cream together the brown sugar and butter until light and fluffy. Mix in the treacle, honey, eggs and vanilla.

4. In a separate bowl, combine the flours, salt, baking powder and bread soda. Mix the dry ingredients into the butter and sugar mixture in three parts, alternating with the buttermilk. Stir in the raspberries and white chocolate.

5. Spoon the batter into the muffin cases, using 115g of batter per muffin. If your batter is firm enough and if using frozen fruit, use an ice cream scoop.

6. Bake in the oven for about 35 minutes, until fully cooked. Remove the muffins from the baking tray to a wire rack to cool.

Cupcakes

For the cupcakes:

240g butter

5 large eggs

240g sugar

280g cream flour

80g self-raising flour

For the fondant icing:

300g prepared white fondant icing

3 drops blue food colouring

3 drops green food colouring

1. Preheat the oven to 190°C.

2. Melt the butter and allow it to cool. Line a muffin tray with paper cases and grease the top of the pan so they don't stick.

3. Whisk the eggs and sugar together until pale and thick. Sieve the flours together and fold into the egg mix. Next pour the butter into the flour and eggs and mix until fully incorporated.

4. Spoon the mix into the paper cases, then bake in the oven for 15–20 minutes. Allow to cool on a wire rack.

5. To make the icing, place the fondant icing in a heatproof bowl and allow to soften over a saucepan of hot water. Add blue and/or green colouring as required in separate bowls. Allow to cool – do not overheat the fondant. Spread the fondant icing over the cooled cupcakes, as required.

Peanut Butter Cookies

115g unsalted butter, softened
115g granulated sugar
85g light brown sugar
130g chunky peanut butter
1 egg, beaten
1 tsp vanilla extract
180g strong white flour
1 tsp baking powder
pinch of salt
60g dark chocolate, chopped
100g toasted peanuts, chopped

1. Preheat the oven to 190°C.

2. Cream the butter, both sugars and peanut butter together until light and fluffy. Gradually add in the egg and vanilla extract.

3. In a separate bowl, sift together the flour, baking powder and salt twice. Add this to the butter mixture along with the chopped chocolate and peanuts. Gently mix until everything has been incorporated. Rest the cookie dough in the fridge for 30 minutes.

4. Remove the dough from the fridge. Lightly dust the countertop and roll the dough into a log, then cut into slices to a thickness of your choosing. Place slices on a baking sheet lined with greaseproof paper or dusted with flour. Bake for 10–12 minutes, or longer if the cookies are cut thick.

5. Remove from oven and place on a wire rack to cool.

Chocolate Chip Cookies

Makes 20 cookies

120g unsalted butter, softened

130g light brown sugar

1 large egg

1 tsp vanilla essence

185g cream flour

½ tsp baking powder

pinch of salt

175g dark Belgian chocolate, chopped

100g milk chocolate, chopped

50g white chocolate, chopped

These cookies are big and chocolatey, and best enjoyed with a coffee in the café.

1. Preheat the oven to 160°C. Grease 2 baking sheets.

2. Beat the butter and sugar together until light and fluffy. Gradually add in the egg and vanilla essence.

3. In a separate bowl, sift the flour together with the baking powder and salt. Add the flour to the butter mix. Mix until all the ingredients combine, then add the chocolates.

4. Place 1 tablespoon of the dough at a time on the baking sheet. Leave plenty of room, as the biscuits will flatten out as they bake.

5. Bake in the oven for 15–18 minutes, depending on size. Cool on a wire rack before storing in an airtight container.

Butter Sponge (Génoise Cake)

150g caster sugar

3 large free-range eggs

150g cream flour

30g melted butter

100g jam

250ml whipped cream

1 punnet strawberries
and/or raspberries (optional)

1. Preheat the oven to 180°C.

2. Place the sugar in a mixing bowl. Adding the egg over a steady stream over a period of about 2 minutes, whisk the eggs and sugar together to a light foam. This will take about 10 minutes using the paddle attachment on a freestanding mixer.

3. Sift in the flour and gently fold it in with your hand. When the flour is almost mixed in, add the melted butter and finish mixing.

4. Divide the mix into 2 x 15cm greased cake tins. Bake for about 20 minutes. Remove and cool the cakes completely on a wire rack.

5. When fully cooled, sandwich the cakes together with a layer of jam and/or cream and fruit in the middle, if desired. Dust the top of the cake with icing sugar.

Note: You can mix the eggs and sugar over a basin of hot water, as this will allow the butter to incorporate more easily into your mix.

Roly's Butter Shortbread

340g butter, softened
115g icing sugar
1 tsp vanilla essence
450g soft flour

1. Preheat the oven to 190°C.

2. Place the butter, icing sugar and vanilla into a mixing bowl. Beat with the paddle attachment, or mix by hand, until all the sugar is incorporated into the butter. Add the flour and mix until you have a shiny, buttery dough that is workable. A good test is to make sure the dough leaves the sides of the bowl clean.

3. Work the dough with your hands to make it pliable, then roll it out into a rectangular shape. Cut out your biscuits in whatever shape you like. Prick the biscuits with a fork and line them out on a baking tray. I like to add a sprinkling of caster sugar to the top before baking.

4. Bake for approximately 12 minutes, depending on the size of the biscuits. They should not colour too much. Allow to cool completely before storing them in an airtight container.

Serves 4–5

Victoria Sponge Sandwich

120g sugar

2 large eggs, beaten

120g unsalted butter, softened

1 tsp vanilla essence

120g cream flour

¼ tsp baking powder

100g jam

250ml whipped cream

1 punnet strawberries
and/or raspberries (optional)
icing sugar, for dusting

*Note: If you want a much
lighter sponge, you should make
this cake using the butter sponge
recipe on p.124.*

1. Preheat the oven to 180°C.

2. Place the sugar in a mixing bowl. Adding the egg in
a steady stream over a period of about 2 minutes, whisk
the eggs and sugar together to a light foam. This will
take about 10 minutes using the paddle attachment
on a freestanding mixer. Add the butter and vanilla
essence. If you want to colour or flavour your sponge
with coffee, caramel or red or pink colouring, for
example, now is the time to add these.

3. In a separate bowl, sieve the flour and baking powder
together and add them into the butter and egg mixture.
It should look like a clear, smooth batter without lumps.

4. Divide the mix into 2 x 15cm greased cake tins.
Bake for about 20 minutes. Remove and cool the cakes
completely on a wire rack.

5. When fully cooled, sandwich the cakes together with
a layer of jam and/or cream and fruit in the middle, if
desired. Dust the top of the cake with icing sugar.

Coffee Gâteau Slice

For the sponge:

150g caster sugar

3 large free-range eggs, beaten

150g cream flour

30g melted butter

**2 tsp ground coffee
or instant coffee granules**

**100g chopped walnuts,
for decorating the top**

For the coffee buttercream:

75ml freshly brewed coffee

240g caster sugar

4 egg whites

120g caster sugar

360g unsalted butter, diced

For the praline:

100g caster sugar

drop of water

100g flaked almonds, toasted

Note: If you would like the
gâteau to be more strongly
flavoured, add 2 tsp coffee
essence when making the
buttercream icing.

This is a delicious gâteau and very popular in the café. I like to finish my coffee gâteau with lots of chopped walnuts and praline.

1. Preheat the oven to 190°C.

2. Place the sugar in a mixing bowl. Adding the egg in a steady stream over a period of about 2 minutes, whisk the eggs and sugar together to a light foam. This will take about 10 minutes using the paddle attachment on a freestanding mixer.

3. Sift in the flour and gently fold it in with your hand. When the flour is almost mixed in, add the melted butter and coffee and finish mixing.

4. Line a Swiss roll tin with greaseproof paper. Pour the batter into the tin and level off evenly with a palette knife. Bake for 10 minutes, until well risen and cooked.

5. Have ready a large sheet of greaseproof paper sprinkled with caster sugar. When the sponge has finished baking, turn it out onto the paper. Remove the paper lining and allow to cool on a wire tray.

6. To make the coffee buttercream, boil the coffee and sugar together until it reaches 118°C on a sugar thermometer. Meanwhile, whisk the egg whites and caster sugar together until shiny and stiff peaks form. Pour in the hot coffee and sugar mixture and continue to whisk until the meringue mixture is cold. This will take about 10 minutes. Whisk the diced butter a little at a time through the meringue mix until it is fully incorporated. Do not stop mixing until a cream is formed. If your mix splits, add some more butter.

7. To make the praline, gently heat the water and sugar until a caramel is formed. Add in the toasted nuts. Be very careful, as the mix will be very hot.

8. Oil a baking sheet and carefully pour the hot caramel out onto the sheet. Allow it to cool, then break into pieces. Crush in a blender or with a rolling pin until it resembles fine breadcrumbs (or a little bigger). Store in a dry, airtight container for up to 6 weeks.

9. Make the gâteau by cutting the sponge into 3 equal lengths. Build up each layer with an equal quantity of coffee buttercream. Finish off the top and sides evenly.

10. Dust the sides with praline and pipe some buttercream on top. Finish with chopped walnuts.

11. Chill the finished gâteau in the fridge, but take it out 2–3 hours before serving to allow it to come to room temperature.

Chocolate Fondant

**230g dark Belgian chocolate
(at least 55% cocoa solids)**

130g butter

2 whole large eggs

1 large egg yolk

100g icing sugar

70g self-raising flour

20g cocoa powder

½ tsp baking powder

icing sugar, for dusting

**pistachio or vanilla ice cream
(see p.167), to serve**

1. Preheat the oven to 160°C.

2. Finely grate 100g of the Belgian chocolate. Butter 6 ramekin moulds, then dust with the grated chocolate. Shake out the excess.

3. Melt the remaining chocolate and butter in a bowl placed over hot water or in a microwave until smooth. Leave to cool for 10 minutes.

4. Using an electric whisk, whisk the eggs, egg yolk and icing sugar together until pale and thick, then incorporate it into the melted chocolate. Sift the flour, cocoa powder and baking powder together, then fold it into the chocolate mixture.

5. Divide the fondant mixture evenly between the moulds and bake for 12 minutes.

6. Turn out the fondant onto plates, dust with icing sugar and serve with pistachio or vanilla ice cream.

Chapter 4

Desserts

Chocolate Mousse

Serves 6–8

**400g dark Belgian chocolate
(at least 55% cocoa solids)**

600ml double cream

2 free-range eggs

35ml Cointreau

This mousse recipe has many different uses, such as for birthday cakes or as a wonderful dessert, or it can be used as a filling for a roulade.

If you do not like dark chocolate, you can use milk chocolate or other flavourings. Nuts can also be added.

1. Bring a small saucepan of water to the boil and melt the chocolate in a heatproof bowl over the simmering water, making sure no water comes in contact with the chocolate. Remove from the heat and set aside.

2. Lightly whip the cream.

3. In another heatproof bowl, whisk the eggs vigorously over the hot water for about 1 minute. Remove from the heat and continue to whisk the eggs until they have cooled and are light and fluffy.

4. Pour the Cointreau over the eggs and fold in. Add the chocolate to the egg mixture and continue to fold. Finally, fold in the cream until a rich mousse is formed. Refrigerate the mousse for 3–4 hours. Serve chilled.

Serves 8

750g mascarpone cheese

120g caster sugar

3 eggs, separated

330ml very strong,
  cold black coffee

200ml Kahlúa or other
  coffee-flavoured liqueur

20ml brandy

24 Savoiardi (Italian sponge
  fingers) or boudoir biscuits

cocoa powder or chocolate
  shavings, to finish

Classic Tiramisu

Tiramisu in Italian means 'pick me up', which refers here to the combination of strong, good coffee and alcohol. This is an incredibly quick and easy recipe to make, but I suggest you make it a full 24 hours beforehand to let the flavours develop. This dessert can be made individually or as a large quantity.

1. Place the mascarpone cheese, sugar and egg yolks into a bowl and whisk together until light and creamy. Whisk the egg whites separately until they form stiff peaks. Fold the egg whites into the mascarpone mixture until everything is incorporated.

2. Mix the coffee and alcohol together in a shallow dish and dip the biscuits in, one at a time. Do not oversoak – to keep their shape, you have to be quick.

3. Place a spoonful of the mascarpone mix on the bottom of your glass or bowl and line with the soaked biscuits. Repeat this process 3 times, finishing with mascarpone mix. Dust the top with cocoa powder or chocolate shavings. Refrigerate for 24 hours and serve chilled.

White Chocolate & Double Chocolate Brownie Trifle

Serves 6

For the white chocolate cream:
500g white chocolate
750ml cream
4 eggs

For the chocolate brownie:
2 eggs
250g sugar
150g butter
65g cocoa powder
65g self-raising flour
50g chocolate chips

For the topping:
2 punnets fresh raspberries
100g grated chocolate

This light, luscious trifle is very quick and easy to make. I like to serve this as individual trifles rather than in a big bowl, so I suggest using tall glasses, like a knicker-bocker glory glass, or wide martini glasses. This dessert is gelatine free and can be made gluten free by replacing the flour with gluten-free flour. Baileys can be added to the white chocolate if desired.

1. Preheat the oven to 170°C.

2. To make the white chocolate cream, melt the chocolate over a saucepan of hot water, making sure the water doesn't touch the chocolate. Lightly whip the cream in a separate bowl. In another bowl, whisk the eggs over a saucepan of hot water until light and fluffy. Do not overcook, or the eggs will scramble. Remove the eggs from the heat and continue whisking for 8 minutes, until cool. Add the melted chocolate to the eggs and fold together. Fold in the semi-whipped cream until a thick yet pourable mix is formed.

3. To make the brownie, whisk the eggs and sugar together until pale and light. Melt the butter in a heavy-bottomed saucepan to boiling point. Allow to cool, then add to the egg and sugar mix. Sieve the cocoa and flour together and fold into the egg mixture. Add in the chocolate chips, then pour into a greased baking tray or muffin tin and bake for 20–30 minutes. Remove from the oven and allow to cool.

4. When cool, dice up the brownie into small, uniform cubes, then place a portion in each of the serving glasses. Pour over the white chocolate cream and allow it to envelop the brownie. Finish with more diced brownie and fresh raspberries and some grated dark chocolate on top.

Irish Whiskey Coffee Cups

For the mocha fudge cake:

1 egg

290g caster sugar

100g dark chocolate

170g butter, diced

170ml water

70ml Kahlúa

50g instant coffee

150g plain flour

2 tbsp self-raising flour

2 tbsp cocoa powder

For the coffee custard:

5 egg yolks

2 eggs

500ml cream

50g sugar

5 tsp coffee essence

For the whiskey cream:

300ml double cream

35ml whiskey, or to taste

1 tbsp cocoa powder or grated
    chocolate, to decorate

This is a favourite of mine for St Patrick's Day. I created this dessert by basing it on the traditional Irish coffee, using mocha fudge cake, coffee custard and Irish whiskey cream. Serve this in a coffee cup or a latte glass.

1. Preheat the oven to 160°C.

2. To make the mocha fudge cake, whisk the egg with the sugar until pale. In a saucepan, melt the chocolate, butter, water, Kahlúa and coffee until smooth. Melt it gently or the chocolate will burn. Allow to cool, then add to the egg and sugar mix.

3. Sift the flours with the cocoa powder and fold them into the chocolate mix.

4. Pour the batter into a small greased tin or baking tray and bake in the oven for 20–30 minutes. Remove from the oven and allow to cool. When completely cool, dice up the cake into even-sized cubes.

5. Reduce the oven temperature to 130°C.

6. To make the coffee custard, gently mix the egg yolks with the whole eggs until combined. In a pot, heat the cream, sugar and coffee essence to about 60°C – do not boil. Pour the cream over the eggs and mix. Strain this

Note: If you want a dry, strong dessert, increase the amount of coffee in the cake and add more whiskey to the cream.

Note: To cook in a bain-marie, place your dishes into a deep tray filled one-third of the way up with warm water. This helps custard and egg-based dishes to cook evenly without burning or scrambling.

liquid through a sieve to remove any shell that may have fallen in.

7. Take the coffee cup or dish you'll be serving the dessert in and pour in the custard halfway up. Place the cups into a deep tray filled one-third of the way up with warm water (a bain-marie). Use cling film to fully cover the tray so as to trap the steam, creating a seal around the tray. Cook in a warm oven at 130°C, until set. Remove from the oven and allow to cool.

8. To assemble, sprinkle the diced sponge over the custard. Lightly whip the cream and add the whiskey. Pour the whiskey cream over the top of the sponge, then dust with cocoa powder or grated chocolate. move to a wire tray to cool.

Roly's Bread & Butter Pudding

Serves 8–10

For the custard:

550ml double cream

50g caster sugar

**1 vanilla pod, split with
 seeds scraped out**

½tsp ground cinnamon

½tsp nutmeg

5 egg yolks

2 eggs

For the bread pudding:

**1 loaf of brioche
 or any white bread**

100g butter, melted

**200g sultanas, soaked
 in hot water & dried**

This pudding has been a popular dessert in England since the thirteenth century. The dessert was first known as Poor Man's Pudding because instead of using milk or cream to soften the stale bread, they used water and then squeezed it dry before adding sugar, spices and other ingredients.

I like to think we have come on since then, but in reality the basics have not changed at all. In Roly's, we like to use a cream-based custard and our own home-baked brioche bread. Once the bread is buttered and toasted before assembling, the dish can be called Bread and Butter Pudding.

1. Preheat the oven to 205°C.

2. Warm the cream, sugar, vanilla pod and seeds, cinnamon and nutmeg in a heavy-bottomed saucepan. Do not boil.

3. In a deep bowl, mix (do not whisk) the eggs and yolks together. Pour the cream into the egg mixture, gradually stirring all the time. Strain the mix into a jug through a fine strainer. Set aside.

4. Trim the crusts off your chosen bread, then cut the loaf into 1¼ cm-thick slices. Place the bread on a baking sheet, brush with melted butter (saving some to grease the baking dish), sprinkle with sugar and toast in the oven for 10 minutes, until golden brown.

5. Brush the pudding dish you are going to use with some melted butter, then sprinkle the dish with sugar.

6. Place a level, single layer of toasted bread in the bottom of the dish. The sides of the bread should touch or overlap so that the bottom is completely covered. Sprinkle half of the sultanas evenly over the bread, then pour on just enough custard to soak the bread. Cover with a second layer of bread and repeat the process. The top layer should just have soaked bread and no sultanas. Allow to stand for a couple of hours to allow the bread to absorb as much custard as possible.

7. Reduce the oven temperature to 170°C.

8. Sprinkle over some caster sugar, cover the dish and bake for 30 minutes in a bain-marie (see note on p.139), then uncovered for a further 30 minutes, or until the pudding is set and the top has turned golden brown.

Roly's Biscuit Cake

400g milk chocolate

250g dark chocolate

200g white chocolate

160g unsalted butter

300g golden syrup

300g digestive biscuits

**ganache for the top,
melted (see p.169)**

This particular cake is one of the best sellers in the café. It combines three different chocolates and sticky golden syrup with crunchy digestive biscuits. It's sweet and very rich when finished with ganache. Different biscuits can be added, but I think the original digestive is best. This cake is best served at room temperature. It can also be made flat and used like a bar.

1. Melt all the chocolates, butter and golden syrup in a bowl over a pot of hot water, making sure the water doesn't touch the chocolate. In a separate bowl, roughly break up the biscuits, though not too small. When the chocolate is fully melted with the butter, add the biscuits into the chocolate and stir until everything is combined.

2. Spread the chocolate digestive mixture in a cake tin or flat baking tray and allow to set in the fridge. After 2 hours, cover the top with melted ganache, then place back into the fridge to set. Remove from the tin, cut into slices or bars and serve.

Baked Vanilla & Blueberry Cheesecake

Serves 8–10

For the biscuit base:

400g digestive biscuits

50g drinking chocolate powder

50g brown sugar

50g toasted nibbed almonds

130g unsalted butter, melted

For the cheesecake mix:

400g full-fat soft cheese (e.g. Philadelphia or mascarpone)

3 eggs, separated

juice of ½ lemon

1 vanilla pod, seeded

½ tsp vanilla essence

350ml double cream

50g caster sugar

2 punnets fresh blueberries

icing sugar, for dusting

1. Preheat the oven to 190°C.

2. To make the biscuit base, crumble the digestives in a bowl, add in the rest of the ingredients and mix well. Put into the base of a 20cm cheesecake ring and press down firmly using the back of a spoon. Place in the fridge to set.

3. To make the cheesecake, beat together the cheese, egg yolks, lemon juice and vanilla seeds for approximately 7 minutes. Gradually beat in the cream until the mix is combined.

4. In a separate bowl, whisk the egg whites until they hold their shape, then add the caster sugar until it forms stiff peaks. Fold the egg whites into the cheese mixture, then add 1 full punnet of blueberries into the mix.

5. Pour the cheese and egg white mixture into the tin over the biscuit base, then bake for 20–30 minutes, until golden brown and set. Allow to cool, then dust with icing sugar and decorate with the remaining blueberries.

Pear, Apple & Blackberry Crumble

Serves 8–10

For the crumble topping:

50g plain cream flour

75g Demerara sugar

50g digestive or any other biscuits, crushed

25g oat flakes

1 tsp mixed spice

75g unsalted butter, diced

For the filling:

40g unsalted butter

4 ripe pears, peeled & cut into wedges

3 apples, peeled & cut into wedges

100g sugar

1 tsp ground cinnamon

1 tsp ground ginger

100ml apple juice

2 tbsp lemon juice

1 tbsp cornflour

2 punnets blackberries

ice cream or custard, to serve

1. Preheat the oven to 190°C.

2. To make the crumble topping, sift the flour into a bowl. Mix in the sugar, biscuits, oat flakes and mixed spice. Gradually work in the butter to make a crumbly mixture.

3. To make the filling, melt the butter in a saucepan and add the pear and apple wedges and sugar, followed by the spices and apple and lemon juices. Cook until the fruit is tender but not fully cooked. Remove from the heat and strain the fruit from the juice.

4. Place the juice back into the saucepan and bring to the boil. In a separate bowl, add a drop of water to the cornflour and stir to form a paste, then add this to the juice to thicken it. When the juice has thickened, add it back to the fruit.

5. Add the blackberries to the cooked fruit and put into an oven-proof serving bowl. Cover the fruit with the crumble topping and bake for 30 minutes, until the top is brown and crunchy. Serve hot with ice cream or fresh custard.

Rice Pudding
with Rhubarb Compote

For the rice pudding:

90g arborio rice, washed

850ml milk

pinch of grated nutmeg

**1 vanilla pod,
  split & seeds scraped**

285ml cream

30g butter

100g condensed milk

For the rhubarb compote:

200ml red wine

100ml raspberry purée

100g caster sugar

100ml orange juice

1 cinnamon stick

pinch of ground ginger

**500g young rhubarb,
  cut into 5cm pieces**

**ice cream or whipped cream,
  to serve**

*Note: The compote can also be
served with other desserts, such
as ice cream or crêpes.*

1. To make the rice pudding, place the washed rice, milk, nutmeg and vanilla pod and seeds into a saucepan over a moderate heat. Stir until the milk starts to boil, then reduce the heat and simmer slowly, stirring frequently, until the rice is cooked. Add in the cream, butter and condensed milk. Stir over the heat, then place in a serving bowl or allow to cool and store in the fridge.

2. To make the compote, put all ingredients except the rhubarb into a saucepan and bring to the boil. Reduce the heat and allow to simmer for 5 minutes. Add in the rhubarb and continue to simmer until the fruit is tender. Leave to cool.

3. Serve hot with ice cream or whipped cream.

Poached Fruits in Cinnamon & Star Anise Syrup

Serves 6–8

For the syrup:

2 litres water

900g caster sugar

1 lemon, cut into wedges

**1 vanilla pod,
  split & seeds scraped**

2 cinnamon sticks

12 whole cloves

6 star anise

2 bay leaves

For the poached fruit:

6 pears

3 apples

10 plums

6 peaches

6 apricots

12 cherries

ice cream or cream, to serve

Note: If you want to make a red wine syrup to poach the fruit in, omit the water and replace it with red wine.

To poach means to cook food gently in liquid at simmering point, so that the surface of the liquid is only just agitated.

1. To make the syrup, combine all the ingredients in a saucepan and bring to the boil. Remove from the heat and set aside. Because all fruits differ in size, shape and texture, different poaching times and techniques will apply.

2. For pears and apples, peel the fruit and place into the syrup, keeping it submerged by using a plate or lid on top, otherwise the fruit will rise to the surface, turn brown and will not cook evenly. Boil gently for about 5 minutes, then lower the heat and gently simmer very slowly until the fruit is tender and cooked all the way through.

3. To poach plums, peaches, apricots, cherries, figs and other soft fruits, add the prepared fruit to the boiling syrup and lower the heat immediately, allowing the mixture to simmer gently for 2 minutes – do not boil!

4. Bring all your poached fruit together in a bowl. Pour over some syrup and serve immediately with ice cream or cream.

Deep Apple Pie with Homemade Custard

Serves 8–10

960g dessert apples, peeled & cored

30g butter

180g sugar

1tsp lemon juice

1tsp ground cinnamon

sweet pastry (see p.157)

l'Anglaise sauce (see p.172) or cream, to serve

Note: Approximately 125g of sultanas may be added to the apple filling, if desired.

1. Preheat the oven to 200°C.

2. Cut the apples into fairly thick slices and place in a saucepan with the butter, sugar, lemon juice and cinnamon. Simmer the apples gently for 2 minutes, until barely cooked. Remove and strain the juice off the apples. Allow to cool.

3. Line a flan ring or tartlet ring with the pastry and fill with the apple mixture. Roll out a pastry disc about 1¼ cm larger than the ring for the top of the pie. Brush the edges of the pastry with water, place the pastry disc over the apple filling and press down on the sides to seal the pie. Cut a slit in the top disc if you like. Sprinkle with caster sugar and bake for 40 minutes.

4. Serve hot with fresh custard and/or cream.

Red Apple Tart Tatin

Makes 4–6

200g caster sugar

1 tbsp water

squeeze of lemon juice

50g butter

6 cloves

5–6 red apples, peeled, cored & sliced

300g puff pastry

whipped double cream, to serve

This is probably one of my favourite apple desserts ever. I remember trying this with Granny Smith apples and it not working out very well. Finally, I tried using red apples because they are a much softer and more absorbent apple, and they caramelised beautifully. Once prepared, this dessert takes just 20 minutes to cook, so it's usually cooked to order, but the results are well worth waiting for.

1. Preheat the oven to 180°C.

2. Mix the sugar, water and lemon juice in a heavy-bottomed saucepan. Bring to the caramel stage or just before (when the mixture reads 154°C–177°C on a sugar thermometer or when it changes to a caramel colour). Pour the caramel into individual tart tatin or blini pans, just covering the bottom. Add a knob of butter and 1 clove to each pan.

3. Place the prepared apples into the caramel (1 apple per pan should do).

4. Roll the puff pastry out to a thickness of 3mm. Cut out circles 2½cm bigger than the pan. Put the pastry on top of the apples and tuck down the sides into the inside of the pan. Place the pans into the hot oven and bake for 20–25 minutes. Remove from the oven and allow to rest for 40 minutes to let the flavours fully develop.

5. To serve, reheat in the oven and turn upside down onto a plate. This dessert is delicious when accompanied by freshly whipped double cream.

Lemon Tart
(Tart au Citron)

Serves 6–8

For the filling:
7 whole eggs
185g caster sugar
2 lemons (grated rind & juice)
60ml lemon juice
265ml double cream
icing sugar, for dusting

For the sweet pastry:
375g unsalted butter
140g icing sugar
4 medium eggs
625g cream flour
1 tsp vanilla essence
1 egg + 4 tbsp milk,
  for the egg wash

1. To make the filling, place all the ingredients into a bowl and gently mix together. Do not aerate. Leave for 2 hours, then strain the mix into a clean container and store until needed.

2. To make the pastry, cream the butter and sugar together in a mixer. Gradually add the eggs over 2 minutes, then add the flour and vanilla. When a pale yellow pastry dough has formed, wrap the pastry in cling film and refrigerate for 30 minutes.

3. Preheat the oven to 210°C.

4. Grease and line a deep 20.5cm flan tin. Roll out the pastry thinly, then place into flan tin. Cover the pastry with greaseproof paper, then fill the base with rice. Bake for 15 minutes, until golden brown. Remove the rice and paper, brush the pastry with the egg wash and place back into the oven for 10 minutes, until fully baked.

5. Reduce the oven temperature to 110°C.

6. Add the lemon tart filling, prepared earlier, and place back in the oven until set.

7. Remove from the oven and allow to cool. Dust liberally with icing sugar and serve.

Fig & Almond Tartine

500g puff pastry

6 fresh figs, sliced

**mascarpone cheese,
  to serve (optional)**

**flaked almonds,
  to serve (optional)**

For the apricot glaze:

100g apricot jam

25ml water

For the almond paste (frangipane):

125g unsalted butter

125g caster sugar

3 medium eggs

½ tsp almond essence

120g ground almonds

25g self-raising flour

20g chopped almonds

1. Preheat the oven to 210°C.

2. To make the apricot glaze, bring the jam and water to the boil in a saucepan, then separate using a strainer.

3. To make the frangipane, cream the butter and sugar together until pale and fluffy. Beat in the eggs and almond essence, then stir in the remaining ingredients until you have a heavy paste.

4. To prepare the tartine, roll out the puff pastry until it's 3mm thick, then use a 12 ½cm cutter or round plate to cut out 4 discs.

5. Place the puff pastry discs on a greased baking sheet. Using a palette knife, spread a thick layer of almond paste onto each pastry disc, starting in the centre and working outwards, leaving the edges uncovered.

6. Place the sliced figs on the pastry in a circular arrangement. Bake for 12–15 minutes, until the pastry is fully cooked.

7. Drizzle apricot glaze liberally over each tartine. Serve with mascarpone cheese and flaked almonds, if desired.

Bakewell Tart

sweet pastry (see p.157)
60g jam
frangipane (see p.159)

For the water icing:
75ml water or stock syrup
240g icing sugar, sieved

Note: To make approx. 1 litre of stock syrup boil 400ml water and 400g sugar together until they form a syrup. You could add star anise, cloves, and orange & lemon zest if you wish.

1. Preheat the oven to 180°C.

2. Line a flan ring with three-quarters of the pastry. Prick the base well with a fork. Spread on the jam. Place the frangipane filling on top of the jam and spread evenly.

3. Roll out the remaining pastry, cut into strips 6mm wide (or use a trellis cutter) and place on top to form a lattice pattern.

4. Bake for 30 minutes, until fully cooked and golden in colour.

5. Meanwhile, to make the water icing, heat the water or stock syrup, then whisk in the sieved icing sugar to form a smooth icing. If it needs to be thinner, add in more water or syrup.

6. When the tart is baked, brush over with thin water icing.

Fresh Summer Berry Pavlova & Passion Fruit Sauce

Serves 6–8

For the pavlova:

3 egg whites

1 tsp white vinegar

175g caster sugar,
  divided in half

1 tsp cornflour, sifted

½ tsp vanilla essence

For the passion fruit sauce:

10 fresh passion fruit

200g caster sugar

500ml passion fruit
  or tropical fruit juice

20g arrowroot (to thicken)

For the topping:

200ml double cream,
  whipped until thick

2 punnets raspberries

2 punnets strawberries

1 punnet redcurrants

*Note: Always leave the oven
door slightly ajar when
cooking pavlova, as steam
will cause it to collapse.*

1. Preheat the oven to 130°C. Line 2 baking sheets with non-stick baking parchment.

2. To make the pavlova, whisk the egg whites with the vinegar in a very clean bowl on the highest speed until they form stiff peaks. Add half of the sugar. Whisk on full speed for about 1 minute, then stop. Mix the other half of the sugar with the cornflour and fold very carefully into the stiff whites using a spatula, taking care not to knock the air out of the mix. Fold in the vanilla essence.

3. Pipe the meringue mixture into small discs on the prepared baking sheets using a plain pastry nozzle. Bake for 55 minutes, or until the meringue bases lift off the paper. Allow to cool before decorating. At this stage, the meringue will probably crack and sink a little. It should be mallowy in the centre.

4. To make the sauce, scrape out all the passion fruit seeds into a saucepan. Add the sugar and the fruit juice and bring to the boil. In a separate cup, add a little water to the arrowroot to make a liquid, then add to boiling syrup until the mixture thickens. Allow the sauce to cool before serving.

5. When the pavlova is cold, spoon on the cream and decorate with the berries. Dust with icing sugar and serve with the passion fruit sauce.

Crêpes

250g strong white flour
55g caster sugar
pinch of salt
4 whole eggs
650ml milk
200ml cream
1 tsp vanilla essence

1. Sift the flour, sugar and salt into a bowl. Add in the eggs and mix into the flour. Gradually add in the milk, cream and vanilla essence. Make sure there are no lumps in the mixture – pass the mix through a sieve to be sure.

2. To cook, heat a lightly oiled non-stick pan and pour in enough crêpe mix to cover the base of the pan (not too thick). Cook over a moderate heat. When one side is cooked, flip over and repeat on the other side. When the crêpe is finished, place it on some greaseproof paper. Continue this process until all the crêpe batter has been used up.

3. Serve hot or cold, lightly sugared, either plain or with your choice of topping, such as roasted plums or apples, sliced bananas, Nutella, ice cream or rhubarb compote (see p.149).

Makes 4–6

Brandy Snap Baskets

30g plain flour
60g caster sugar
pinch of ground ginger
30g unsalted butter
2 tbsp golden syrup

1. Preheat the oven to 190°C.

2. Mix the flour, sugar and ginger together in a bowl.

3. In a saucepan, slowly heat the butter and golden syrup together. Do not boil – just melt. Pour the melted syrup and butter into the flour and mix until a paste is formed.

4. Divide the mixture into 4–6 balls, depending on the size you want. Place the balls onto a greased baking tray (or better still, use silicone mats if you have them). They will spread, so bake them 2 at a time for about 7–8 minutes, until golden brown.

5. Allow to cool for 1 minute, then shape them over a mould to create a basket shape. Leave till they set hard. If they harden before you can shape them, return them to the oven to soften.

6. When your baskets are ready, you can fill them with ice cream, fruit or even chocolate mousse.

Cinnamon Palmiers

Makes 24

100g caster sugar

4 tsp ground cinnamon

400g puff pastry

**cinnamon-flavoured icing
sugar, to dust**

These are very nice when served with ice cream.

1. Preheat the oven to 220°C.

2. Mix the sugar and cinnamon together and set aside.

3. Roll out the puff pastry on a lightly floured surface into a rectangular shape measuring 30.5cm x 100cm. Lightly brush the surface with a drop of water. Sprinkle the cinnamon sugar on liberally, covering the surface. Roll one side of the pastry like a Swiss roll into the centre. Turn the pastry and do the same with the other half.

4. Cut into slices, equal in size. Place the palmiers onto a well-greased baking sheet and flatten them slightly with the palm of your hand. Place another baking sheet on top so they are sandwiched between the 2 baking sheets.

5. Bake for 8–10 minutes, then turn over and bake on the other side for 6 minutes.

6. Remove from the oven and allow to cool on a wire rack. Dust with cinnamon-flavoured icing sugar.

Makes 1½ litres

Vanilla Ice Cream

300ml cream

300ml milk

150g caster sugar

**30g liquid glucose
(confectioner's syrup)**

**1 vanilla pod,
split & seeds scraped out**

9 large egg yolks

1. Place the cream, milk, sugar, glucose and vanilla into a saucepan and bring to the boil. In a separate, heatproof bowl, gently whisk the egg yolks, pour over the scalded milk and mix well together until a thick custard forms. Place the bowl on top of a pot of boiling water and thicken the custard until it coats the back of a wooden spoon.

2. Place the mixture in the fridge to cool for 1–1½ hours, then pour it into an ice cream machine and churn until a smooth ice cream is formed. Store in the freezer.

Serves 4

Sabayon

75g sugar
1 glass white wine
1 leaf gelatine
100ml cold water
4 eggs, separated
125g cream cheese
125ml cream, lightly whipped

Sabayon is similar to Italian Zabaglione.

1. Place half the sugar in a saucepan with the white wine and bring to the boil. Soften the gelatine in cold water and add to the wine and sugar.

2. In a mixer, whisk the egg yolks and cream cheese, then gradually incorporate the wine and sugar mix. Allow the mix to become totally cool before stopping the mixer – this will take about 10 minutes.

3. In another bowl, whisk the egg whites with the remainder of the sugar until they form stiff peaks.

4. Fold the egg whites into the cream cheese mixture, followed by the cream. Leave in the fridge for approximately 30 minutes before use.

Dessert Sauces

Makes ½ litre

185ml cream

30g unsalted butter

40g liquid glucose

185g good-quality dark Belgian chocolate chips (70% cocoa solids)

Chocolate Ganache

1. In a saucepan, bring the cream, butter and glucose to the boil. Pour over the chocolate chips and whisk until a sauce is formed. If it sets, it can be microwaved down again.

Makes 750ml

455g caster sugar

60ml water

1 tsp lemon juice

2 tbsp liquid glucose

360ml double cream

55g unsalted butter

Caramel Sauce

1. Place the sugar, water and lemon juice in a small saucepan and bring to the boil. Add the glucose and cook until it reaches a golden caramel colour.

2. Turn off the heat and pour in the cream (at arm's length, as the sauce may rise and spatter) and stir. If there are any lumps, return to the heat and cook until they are dissolved. Finally, stir in the butter. Add more water if you want a thinner sauce.

Chocolate
Choux

l'Anglaise Sauce

Makes 400ml

30g caster sugar
2 egg yolks
300ml milk
1 tsp vanilla essence
  or ½ vanilla pod

1. Whisk the sugar and egg yolks together. In a saucepan, bring the milk to the boil and stir it into the egg mixture. Pour the egg mixture into a saucepan and stir on a low heat until the sauce coats the back of a spoon (do not allow it to boil). Pass the mixture through a fine strainer and add the vanilla essence. If using a vanilla pod add this to the milk when boiling.

Raspberry Sauce

Makes 350ml

200g fresh or frozen raspberries
100ml water
30g caster sugar
½ cinnamon stick
1 clove
1 star anise

1. Boil all the ingredients to a pulp in a heavy-bottomed saucepan. Blend in a mixer and strain through a sieve to remove the seeds. Place in the fridge and allow to cool. Sweeten to taste.

Rum & Raisin Sauce

Makes 750ml

caramel sauce (see p.169)
50m dark rum
120g raisin

1. Make the caramel sauce. Poach the raisins for about 2 minutes in boiling water, strain and pat dry. Mix the rum into the caramel sauce and add the raisins.

Lemon Curd

Makes approx. 375g

225g caster sugar
50g butter
2 eggs, lightly beaten
zest & juice of 3 lemons

1. Put all the ingredients into the top of a double saucepan or in a basin standing in a pan of simmering water. Stir until the sugar has dissolved. Continue heating, stirring from time to time, until the curd thickens. Strain using a fine sieve and allow to cool in the refrigerator until needed. For orange curd, simply replace the lemons with oranges.

Mango Coulis

Makes 425ml

150ml water
60g caster sugar
1 large, ripe mango,
  peeled, stoned & chopped
1 tsp lemon juice

1. Put the water and sugar into a saucepan and heat gently until the sugar is dissolved. Leave to cool.

2. Using a liquidiser, blend the mango with the lemon juice and cooled sugar syrup, then pass through a fine sieve.

3. Store in clean, airtight jars in the refrigerator, or freeze until required.

Chapter 5

STOCKS, SAUCES & DRESSINGS

Beef Stock

2.5kg beef bones
100ml vegetable oil
2 onions, peeled & chopped
4 carrots, peeled & chopped
4 celery stalks, chopped
8 cloves garlic, peeled
4 tbsp tomato purée
½ bottle red wine
8 litres hot water
1 sprig thyme
1 sprig rosemary
10 black peppercorns

1. Preheat the oven to 200°C.

2. Roast the beef bones in a roasting tray for 30–45 minutes, until golden brown.

3. In a large saucepan, sweat all the vegetables and garlic in the oil for 10 minutes, then turn up the heat and stir constantly, until they turn golden brown. Add the tomato purée and cook for 2 minutes, then add the red wine, water, roasted bones, herbs and peppercorns. Bring to the boil and simmer for 8–10 hours, skimming occasionally. Pass through a sieve into a clean pot and boil to reduce by half.

4. This can be stored in the fridge for 1 week or frozen for up to 3 months.

Fish Stock

1 onion,
  peeled & finely chopped

4 cloves garlic, peeled

2 celery stalks, finely chopped

1 tbsp vegetable oil

1kg white fish bones,
  washed (sole is best)

150ml white wine

2 litres water

1 star anise

1. Fry the onion, garlic and celery in the oil without colouring for 5–10 minutes, until soft. Add the washed fish bones and cook slowly for 5 minutes more. Add the wine and reduce slightly. Add the water and star anise and bring to the boil, skimming well.

2. Simmer gently for 20 minutes, then pass through a sieve and leave to cool. The fish stock can be kept in the fridge for 1–2 days or in the freezer for 1 month.

Makes enough for 4 fish pies (see p.52)

Fish Cream

1 litre fish stock (see above)

½ litre cream

1. Bring the fish stock to the boil and simmer until it has reduced in volume by one-third. Add the cream and simmer until reduced again by one-third.

Chicken Stock

Makes approx. 1 litre

1kg chicken carcasses, chopped

2 litres water

8 celery stalks, chopped

1 onion, chopped

1 leek, chopped

2 cloves garlic

1 sprig thyme

1 bay leaf

1. Put the chicken carcasses in a large pot, add the water and bring to the boil. Skim off all the foam. Add the remaining ingredients and return to the boil, then simmer for 1½–2 hours, skimming off any fat that rises to the top.

2. Pass the stock through a colander, then through a fine strainer. This will keep in the fridge for 1 week or in the freezer for 3 months.

Tomato Relish

Makes 10 portions

1 onion

4 tomatoes, finely chopped

1 red pepper, deseeded & chopped

5 tbsp white wine vinegar

5 tbsp sugar

½ tsp chopped chilli

½ tsp chopped fresh ginger

1 tbsp tomato purée

1 x 400g tin chopped tomatoes, strained

1. Put the onion, tomatoes, pepper, vinegar, sugar, chilli, ginger and tomato purée into a blender and blend together. Place this mixture into a pot, add the strained tomatoes and simmer for 30–40 minutes. This will keep for 1 week in the fridge.

Red Onion Marmalade

Serves 4

30g butter
2 red onions, finely sliced
400ml red wine
25g sugar
100ml red wine vinegar

1. Melt the butter in a saucepan and add the red onions. Cook slowly for about 30 minutes on a low heat, stirring occasionally, until soft. Add the red wine and reduce until nearly dry, then add the sugar and red wine vinegar. Continue to cook until the mixture is nearly dry. This will keep for 1 week in the fridge.

Basil Pesto

Makes approx. 300ml

60g basil leaves
30g parsley
30g pine nuts
15g walnuts
2 cloves garlic,
   peeled & chopped
250ml olive oil
salt & freshly ground
   black pepper

1. Put the herbs, pine nuts, walnuts and garlic in a food processor. Add half the oil and process until the ingredients are finely chopped. With the processor running, gradually add the remaining oil. Season to taste.

Note: Put pesto in a plastic squeeze bottle and use it for decorating a plate.

Serves 4

Roast Garlic Dressing

4 cloves garlic, peeled

**salt & freshly ground
  black pepper**

1 egg yolk

1 tsp Dijon mustard

100ml white wine vinegar

400ml olive oil

1. Preheat the oven to 190°C.

2. Season the garlic cloves with salt and pepper. Wrap in tinfoil and bake for 45 minutes, until soft.

3. In a bowl, whisk the egg yolk, mustard and white wine vinegar together.

4. Remove the garlic from the tinfoil and crush to a paste. Add the crushed garlic to the egg mixture, then slowly whisk in the olive oil. Season to taste. This will keep for 5 days in the fridge.

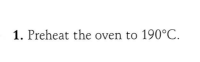

Index